COVENANTS *of* ISRAEL

The Messiah and the COVENANTS of ISRAEL

Bryan W Sheldon

By: Bryan W. Sheldon
Copyright © Bryan W. Sheldon 2009
GOSPEL FOLIO PRESS
All Rights Reserved

Published by
GOSPEL FOLIO PRESS
304 Killaly St. W.
Port Colborne, ON L3K 6A6
CANADA

ISBN: 978 192 676 5105

Cover design by Rachel Brooks
All Scripture quotations from the
King James Version unless otherwise noted.

Printed in USA

CONTENTS

Introduction

One of the great foundation blocks of the healthy relationship between God and humankind is His righteousness. It can be guaranteed that in all His speech and actions He is righteous. By this I suggested that because He is righteous you can trust what He says, you can trust His word.

Invariably, He says what He means, and He means what He says.

Every word that comes from the mouth of God is carefully chosen and perfectly weighted. And because of His foreknowledge, He never, at any time, has to reverse or cancel His promises. In these days when there are subtle attempts to undermine the Word of God, we declare we can trust it, all of it, with no exceptions, and this is especially true of those utterances of the LORD that have covenant status. We have confidence in the righteousness of God, and confidence in the Word of God, and confidence in the covenant promises of God.

Inasmuch as the New Covenant was a guaranteed promise to Israel we must ask how it applies to Gentile believers. But since a proper understanding of the subject will necessitate an examination of the whole covenant relationship between God and Israel we will also examine the Abrahamic, Mosaic, Land and Davidic Covenants.

Chapter 1
The Glory of God

God's prime purpose – to work all things for His own glory. Renald E. Showers wrote: "The Bible deals with the issue of meaning. It offers a systematic interpretation of history. It covers the entire scope of history from beginning to end, including the what and why of the future. It presents a unifying principle which ties together and makes sense of the whole gamut of events, distinctions, and successions. **The Bible demonstrates that history has an ultimate goal or purpose**"[1] (emphasis added). If this is true, what is that ultimate goal? Normally, there is offered two answers to this question. The first is that God's ultimate goal in His dealings with humankind is redemptive, that is, He is working for the salvation of man. The second is that God is working all things for His own glory. In the first it appears that humanity is central, that is, *"all things work together for good to those who love God, to those who are the called according to His purpose"* (Rom. 8:28). In the second, it makes God and His glory central. It seems to this writer that the second is more credible than the first, that is, that God is working all things for His own glory. That it would include a plan of salvation for fallen humanity within its remit is quite understandable, but ultimately all will be accomplished for the glory of God. Paul, in his epistle to the Corinthians, spoke of the hardships he endured in discharging the duties entailed in the stewardship of the gospel. He wrote, *"For all things are for your sakes"* (2 Cor. 4:15), which on the face of it would support the view of those that say that the purpose of God is mainly salvific; but Paul makes that view secondary, and puts the glory of God in prime place, for he continued, *"that grace, having spread through*

---

1   Renald E. Showers, <u>There Really Is a Difference</u> (Bellmawr, NJ: Friends of Israel Gospel Ministry, 1990)

*the many, **may cause thanksgiving to abound to the glory of God**"* (emphasis added). Similarly, in Ephesians, he states that events within the predetermined will of God is in harmony with this over-riding aim that all things should redound to His glory. Paul wrote, *"having predestined us to adoption as sons by Jesus Christ to Himself, according to the good pleasure of His will, **to the praise of the glory of His grace**, by which He made us accepted in the Beloved"* (Eph 1:5-6, emphasis added). The essence of this is repeated in verses 11 through 14. *"In Him also we have obtained an inheritance, being predestined according to the purpose of Him who works all things according to the counsel of His will, that we who first trusted in Christ **should be to the praise of His glory**. In Him you also trusted, after you heard the word of truth, the gospel of your salvation; in whom also, having believed, you were sealed with the Holy Spirit of promise, who is the guarantee of our inheritance until the redemption of the purchased possession, **to the praise of His glory.**"* To the Philippians he wrote: *"And this I pray, that your love may abound still more and more in knowledge and all discernment, that you may approve the things that are excellent, that you may be sincere and without offense till the day of Christ, being filled with the fruits of righteousness which are by Jesus Christ, **to the glory and praise of God**"* (Phil. 1:9-11, emphasis added).

These verses teach that we are saved to the glory of God, and we are being kept to the glory of God, and our lives should be lived to the glory of God.

Indeed Paul encapsulates it in a phrase, *"do all **to the glory of God**"* (1 Cor. 10:31). Christians for centuries have known this. The Westminster shorter catechism asks the question, "What is the chief end of man?" and gives the answer, "Man's chief end is to glorify God and to enjoy Him forever". It supports the first half of this answer (man's chief end is to glorify God) with the following proof texts:

"I will praise You, O Lord my God, with all my heart, And I will glorify Your name forevermore" (Ps 86:12).

"Also your people shall all be righteous; They shall inherit the land forever, The branch of My planting, The work of My hands, That I may be glorified" (Isa. 60:21).

"For of Him and through Him and to Him are all things, to whom be glory forever. Amen" (Rom. 11:36).

"For you were bought at a price; therefore glorify God in your body and in your spirit, which are God's" (1 Cor. 6:20).

"Therefore, whether you eat or drink, or whatever you do, do all to the glory of God" (1 Cor. 10:31).

"You are worthy, O LORD, *To receive glory and honor and power; For You created all things, And by Your will they exist and were created"* (Rev. 4:11).

If you add the verse, *"The heavens declare the glory of God; And the firmament shows His handiwork"* (Ps. 19:1), then it could be suggested that we should also look after the planet to the glory of God.

Is There a Definition of the Glory of God?

But the concept, 'the glory of God,' is very difficult to get a handle on. The phrase is used in so many ways and in so many contexts that no one definition seems adequate. But there is an incident in the Bible where the main features of the 'glory of God' are identified, and so can provide us with a limited definition which may help. During a dispensation-changing encounter when God provided a legal framework for the nation of Israel, Moses asked God for a glimpse of His glory. In acceding to this request the LORD first described what would happen, and then fulfilled it exactly as He described it. The experience was clearly tailored to suit the need of Moses, and indicated how the glory of the LORD related to humankind. In it, God's glory was tied up with His Name and His goodness. When the LORD appeared, He proclaimed what the rabbis came to call the 'Thirteen Attributes of Mercy' (Hebrew - *Shelosh Hesreh Middot*).[2] *"The* LORD, *the* LORD *God, merciful and gracious, longsuffering, and abounding in goodness and truth, keeping mercy for thousands, forgiving iniquity and transgression and sin"* (Ex. 34:6-7). Only after

---

2   See comment in Exodus (Sarna, N.M.) the JPS Torah Commentary (216). (Philadelphia: Jewish Publication Society, 1991)

11

the thirteen attributes of mercy does He mention the attribute of justice, *"by no means clearing the guilty, visiting the iniquity of the fathers upon the children and the children's children to the third and the fourth generation"* (Ex. 34:7). In His relationship with humankind, God must exercise righteous judgment, but He delights in showing mercy. In these verses, His magnanimous qualities are emphasized over His judgmental actions. He demonstrated this priority once and for all by sending the Messiah, His own Son, to take the judgment called for by His own righteousness, and to provide mercy for all who would receive it.

So, in His relationship with humankind, it is the Lord's mercy that provides the beating heart of His glory. He certainly made sure that Moses knew exactly the qualities that expressed His glory most fully. *"Goodness and truth"* could equally be translated *"Kindness and faithfulness"*. The Hebrew *Hesed ve-emet* appears frequently as a word pair[3] to express a single concept. Each of the components has a wide range of meaning. *Hesed* involves acts of beneficence, mutuality, and often also obligations that flow from a legal relationship. *Hemet,* usually translated "truth," encompasses reliability, durability, and faithfulness. The combination of terms expresses God's absolute and eternal dependability in dispensing His benefactions.[4] They are enumerated - mercy, grace, longsuffering, and forgiveness for iniquity, transgression and sin. (These last three are the Biblical descriptors that are used to summarize all kinds of sin – sins of word, sins of thought, sins of deed, sins of commission, sins of omission, secret sins and open sins, accidental sins and presumptuous sins, deliberate sins and unintentional sins, sins against man and sins against God, sinful motives that produce sinful actions as well as the sinful actions themselves.) Having said, *"I will make all My goodness pass before you, and I will proclaim the name of the Lord before you. I will be gracious to whom I will be*

---

3   Cf. Gen. 24:27, 49; 32:11; 47:29; Josh. 2:14; 2 Sam. 2:6; 15:20; Ps. 25:10; 40:11; 57:4; 61:8; 85:11; 86:15; 89:15; 115:1; 138:2; Prov. 3:3; 14:22; 16:6; 20:28.

4   See comment in Exodus (Sarna, N.M.) the JPS Torah Commentary (216). (Philadelphia: Jewish Publication Society, 1991)

gracious, and I will have compassion on whom I will have compassion" (Ex. 33:19), the act is described more fully in its performance. Its structure was something like the custom of Eastern potentates who would send a herald before them to announce their name, attributes and high ranking titles. *"Now the Lord descended in the cloud and stood with him there, and proclaimed the name of the Lord. And the Lord passed before him and proclaimed, 'The Lord, the Lord God, merciful and gracious, longsuffering, and abounding in goodness and truth, keeping mercy for thousands, forgiving iniquity and trans-gression and sin, by no means clearing the guilty, visiting the iniquity of the fathers upon the children and the children's children to the third and the fourth generation'"* (Ex. 34:5-7). It is clear that both righteousness and mercy are elements of His glory, but if righteousness is the foundation, mercy is the capstone. As James wrote: *"Mercy triumphs over judgment"* (Jas. 2:13).

The Name of God used in the proclamation of His goodness is the identifier that is considered by the Hebrew nation as the holiest and most Jewish of all God's Names. It is written with four consonants YHWH (*yud, hei, vav, hei*) and is referred to as the *Tetragrammaton* (Greek for 'four letter word'), or the 'Ineffable Name of God', sometimes reduced to '*Ha-Shem*' (the Name). This Name is the Name that takes precedence in the relationship of God with humankind, and stresses the divine qualities of loving kindness and mercy. It is the Name strongly connected to the covenant relationship between the Lord and Israel. It reappears again and again in those compound names that are so precious, i.e. *Jehovah-Jireh; Jehovah-Nissi; Jehovah-Tzid-kenu*; although the use of '*Jehovah*' is the result of using the vowels of '*Adonai*' with the *Tetragrammaton* to be able to pronounce the Name that had ceased to be verbalised after the fall of the Temple in A.D. 70.

Moses, the man, who was the mediator of a covenant of works, asked to see the glory of God and was granted to see a manifestation of the goodness, grace, mercy, truth, longsuffering and forgiveness of God, which was integrally bound up in His Name. We are reminded of the connection with the Decalogue, *"You shall not take the name of the Lord your God in vain, for the Lord will not hold him guiltless who takes His name in vain"*

(Ex. 20:7). Moses, the man whose work is synonymous with legalism and justice, was reminded that mercy is His glory. So even as far back in the *T'nach* as Moses, we are impelled to consider that the LORD's dealings with man, in grace and gift, were to His own glory.

The Shekinah Glory

But goodness and grace, though vocalized, and perhaps accompanied with the noise of trumpets as were other declarations of the LORD, could not be seen by Moses. To complete the encounter, God in His grace provided a visible expression of His presence to accompany the declaration. Moses was allowed to see the 'after-glow' of the *Shekinah*, the outward manifestation of the glory of God revealed in terms of light and colour. The word '*Shekinah*' means 'that which dwells', and was used by the Rabbis to refer to the visible presence of God among men. Repeatedly in the Old Testament we come across the idea that there were certain times when God's glory was visible. In the desert, before the giving of the manna, the children of Israel *"looked toward the wilderness, and behold, the glory of the LORD appeared in the cloud"* (Ex. 16:10). Before the giving of the Ten Commandments, *"the glory of the LORD rested on Mount Sinai"* (Ex. 24:16). When the Tabernacle had been erected and equipped, the glory of the LORD filled it.[5] Other instances of the manifestation of God's glory include the time when Solomon's Temple was dedicated.[6] These were localized terrestrial manifestations of something that was essentially celestial. Ezekiel in his ecstasy saw *"the likeness of the glory of the LORD"* (Ezek. 1:28). In the Old Testament the glory of the LORD came at times when God was very close.

While, for Moses, the passing by of a physical manifestation of the presence of God was but the work of a moment, the whole encounter lasted some six weeks, at the end of which he returned to report back to the Hebrew nation. The Bible tells us that his face shone with the glory of God, and that he had to

---

5   Ex. 40:34
6   1 Kings. 8:11

wear a veil before the elders of Israel would approach him.[7]

So we have two main aspects of the glory of the LORD - the inherent element which is the fusion between mercy and righteousness; and the radiated element which falls on our sight in terms of light and colour. But there is also a more abstract element presented in Scripture. Let's take two examples, one from the Old Testament and one from the New.

The Glory of God and Job

Job, great man that he was, was distressed in his situation and condition; and who wouldn't be? He had lost his family, his possessions and his health. He felt he had a legitimate complaint against God. He thought, "why is this happening to me? If I could find Him I would argue my case, I would explain to Him that this is unfair". What he did not realize was that God was working out things for His own glory. He did finally meet with God, but the wisdom of God silenced him. The LORD said, *"Where were you when I laid the foundations of the earth? Tell Me, if you have understanding. Who determined its measurements? Surely you know! Or who stretched the line upon it? To what were its foundations fastened? Or who laid its cornerstone, When the morning stars sang together, And all the sons of God shouted for joy?"* (Job 38:4-7). In other words, when I created the world I had a purpose and a plan, and I am still working to that higher purpose and I want you to get on board. The higher purpose was, of course, His own glory, of which Job was a part. For it began with, *"Have you considered My servant Job, that there is none like him on the earth, a blameless and upright man, one who fears God and shuns evil?"* (Job 1:8). In other words, Job had been living his life to the glory of God. Yet the actions of a wise God would refine and purify Job's testimony to bring even more glory to Himself. God was accomplishing something in the life of Job through suffering that perhaps could not be accomplished in any other way, simultaneously humbling Satan while revealing His own wisdom.

In Job's situation, if you considered the catalogue of calamities from his point of view, things were difficult to understand.

---

7   Ex. 34:33-35

But if you considered events from God's point of view then they had a completely different complexion. Job was being educated to have a more elevated perspective – to understand more of the character of God. In the first two chapters of the book God is introduced and referred to by His name YHWH. In the middle section (the main argument) Job and his four friends all refer to God by His Name *'Elohim'*. If, as many suggest, Job is a very ancient book, it is likely that Job, in the first instance, did not know God as YHWH. However, by the time we come to the end of the book, he is brought to know God by His covenant Name because, in the last chapters, it is the LORD YHWH that answers. By the end of the experience, Job had been educated to know God better, and to understand something more of His ways. He has learned that God's mathematics is superior - that by subtraction you can increase. And Job, through his suffering also learned to appreciate the infinite wisdom of God, through which Satan was defeated and the LORD glorified.

The end for him was compensating. It turned out to be twice as good as the beginning, and both celestial and terrestrial realms were brought to marvel at the way God ordered all aspects of the experience to redound to His own praise and glory. We must ever remember that the throne room of heaven is central, even for us earthlings. *"The Most High God rules in the kingdom of men"* (Dan. 5:17, 21). Daniel also served the Most High God, but it did not immunize him from calamity. Like Daniel, we need to see things from heaven's point of view, through heaven's eyes.

The Glory of God and Paul

As we turn to the example of Paul, we must make mention of a fundamental difference in their experiences. While Job was a reluctant participant in the drama which defeated Satan, Paul embraced his part. Like Job, Paul's life, viewed from a human perspective, was a long succession of calamities. His experience testifies to a life of difficulties; *"in labours more abundant, in stripes above measure, in prisons more frequently, in deaths often. From the Jews five times I received forty stripes minus one. Three times I was beaten with rods; once I was stoned; three times I was shipwrecked; a night and a day I have been in the deep; in journeys often, in perils of waters, in perils of robbers, in perils of my own countrymen, in perils of the Gentiles, in perils in the city, in perils in the wilderness, in perils in the sea, in perils among false brethren; in weariness and toil, in sleeplessness often, in hunger and thirst, in fastings often, in cold and nakedness— besides the other things, what comes upon me daily: my deep concern for all the churches"* (2 Cor. 11:23-29). Earlier in his letter he offered some reason for it. He wrote: *"We are hard-pressed on every side, yet not crushed; we are perplexed, but not in despair; persecuted, but not forsaken; struck down, but not destroyed— always carrying about in the body the dying of the* LORD *Jesus,"* (2 Cor. 4:8-10). Why? *"…that the life of Jesus also may be manifested in our body."* But the overarching reason was - *"For all things are for your sakes, that grace, having spread through the many, may cause thanksgiving to abound* **to the glory of God**" (2 Cor. 4:15, emphasis added). Paul acknowledged that while he remained faithful to the will of God, all that happened to him and all that he accomplished would be to the glory of the LORD.

The Glory of God and the Celestial

Glory is an intrinsic quality of God. It belongs to Him as light and heat belong to the sun. Unfallen angels, together with the redeemed in heaven, sing His praises and acknowledge His glory. The first words uttered by the heavenly host at the unveiling of the Saviour of the world were *"Glory to God in the highest, And on earth peace, goodwill toward men!"* (Luke 2:14). It is a sin of enormous proportions to withhold from Him a proper acknowledgement of His glory. He suffers injustice if any of His created beings do not recognize His worthiness. Satan said, *"I will ascend into heaven, I will exalt my throne above the stars of God; I will also sit on the mount of the congregation, on the farthest sides of the north; I will ascend above the heights of the clouds, I will be like the Most High,"* (Isa. 14:13-14) but God declared: *"I am the* LORD, *that is My name; And My glory I will not give to another"* (Isa. 42:8). That which is of prime importance to angels is not their relation to the inhabitants of earth, but rather their service to God. In other words, for all celestial beings, God is the centre of their world, not man. Theirs is primarily a service of worship that understands the ineffable majesty and glory of God, and which, because of the infinity of the worthiness of God, continues without ceasing forever. John states that in their worship the living creatures: *"rest not day and night, saying, 'Holy, holy, holy, LORD God Almighty, which was, and is, and is to come'"* (Rev. 4:8). Isaiah asserts that they *"cried one unto another, and said, Holy, holy, holy, is the LORD of hosts: the whole earth is full of His glory"* (Isa. 6:3). Their humility, suggested by the covering of their feet,[8] is natural since they are ever before Him whose majesty and glory is transcendent. The ministry of angels to the Godhead is no small thing, and inasmuch as they ministered to Jesus, it speaks volumes as to His deity. The birth, life, death, resurrection, and ascension of Christ were to the angels, stupendous realities. It is of no small consequence that, as stated by the Apostle, Christ, while here on the earth, *"was seen of angels"* (1 Tim. 3:16).

The Glory of God and the Terrestrial

The problem, of course, was that generally, humankind was unable to appreciate God's glory properly. Like the glory of the sun, it was only observed from afar. While the glory of the LORD was unknown to most, some were able to see the outworking of it, that is, the hand of the LORD in blessing. But everything changed with the coming of the Son of God. He has brought the glory of God close to man without endangering him. *"And the Word was made flesh, and dwelt among us, (and we beheld **His glory, the glory as of the only begotten of the Father**,) full of grace and truth"* (John 1:14, emphasis added). As was revealed to Moses, the essence of the glory of God is that He is full of grace and truth. The glory of Jesus is that He is full of grace and truth. If we imitate Moses and ask God for a glimpse of His glory, He will direct us to Jesus. *"For God, who commanded the light to shine out of darkness, hath shined in our hearts, to give the light of the knowledge **of the glory of God** in the face of Jesus Christ"* (2 Cor. 4:6, KJV, emphasis added). Jesus is , *"... **the brightness of His glory**, and the express image of His person"* (Heb. 1:3).

---

8   Isa. 6:2

This dispensation is perhaps the most privileged of all, for both Jew and Gentile are encouraged to work for the glory of God. And those that are engaged in this pursuit will meditate much on the LORD Jesus, and the more they consider His attributes and the more they understand His character, the more they will perceive His glory. And then the object of their affection will in turn affect them. *"But we all, with unveiled face, beholding as in a mirror* **the glory of the LORD***, are being transformed into* **the same image from glory to glory***, just as by the Spirit of the LORD"* (2 Cor. 3:18, emphasis added). And as they acknowledge the worth and worthiness of their Master, they will foreshadow that great congregational act that is yet to come when every tongue will, *"confess that Jesus Christ is LORD,* **to the glory of God** *the Father"* (Phil. 2:11, emphasis added). Those that work to the glory of God are on course to share in the glory of God. *"Therefore we do not lose heart. Even though our outward man is perishing, yet the inward man is being renewed day by day. For our light affliction, which is but for a moment, is working for us a far more exceeding and eternal weight of glory"* (2 Cor. 4:16-19).

The Glory of God and Jesus

For those who wish to make a difference for good in this world the example of the Saviour is the highest that can be viewed. Jesus did all for the glory of God. And since the mercy of God, which we have identified as being an essential element of the glory of God, depends on the substitutionary death of Jesus to satisfy the aspect of justice and righteousness which is also involved, then the death of Christ must be seen in terms of the glory of God. This is exactly so, and the closer Jesus got to His judicial execution the more this aspect of His service was emphasized. His death and resurrection were to be, for His contemporary generation, the sign of the prophet Jonah. The raising of Lazarus from Hades was orchestrated in such a way that it was an initial example of the sign. Before Lazarus had died, but in anticipation of the final result, Jesus said, *"This sickness is not unto death, but for* **the glory of God***, that the* **Son of God may be glorified through it"** (John 11:4, emphasis added). Of course, to complete the sign of the prophet Jonah, Lazarus had to be dead three days and three nights. So when Jesus finally arrived at the tomb and commanded that it should be opened, practical Martha was compelled to raise an objection to the actions of the LORD. His response was to return to the information that He had recently provided. He said, *"Did I not say to you that if you would believe you would see* **the glory of God***?"* (John 11:40, emphasis added). So the raising of Lazarus, the act that would pre-figure His own resurrection, as well as being the most vivid illustration of His assertion, *"I am the resurrection"*, was identified as being a demonstration of the glory of God.

This was further enforced when, in Passion Week, certain visitors to Jerusalem asked for an audience. Jesus saw in their request a further indication of His mission and again referred to His sacrificial death. He said, *"The hour has come that* **the Son of Man should be glorified***. Most assuredly, I say to you, unless a grain of wheat falls into the ground and dies — it remains alone; but if it dies, it produces much grain,"* (John 12:23-24, emphasis added) adding *"Now My soul is troubled, and what shall I say? 'Father, save Me from this hour?' But for this purpose I came to this hour. Father,* **glorify Your name'***"* (John 12:27, 28, emphasis added). In other words, let this act of obedience be to the glory of the Father. An assurance was given in a *Bat Kohl*.[9] *"I have both glorified it and will glorify it again"* (John 12:28). The Father had accepted it as such and assured His Son that the work accomplished by His death would redound to the glory of the Godhead again and again and again. This was re-enforced for the disciples on Passover evening when Peter and John visited the Temple to kill a Lamb that was without blemish – a Lamb that was to once again typify the death of the Lamb of God that would take away the sin of the world. The blood which was dashed against the altar was first caught in a golden vessel, gold signifying the glory of God.

Then again, on the night in which He was betrayed, Jesus prayed: *"I have glorified You on the earth. I have finished the work which You have given Me to do"* (John 17:4).

---

9   A word from heaven

So we return to our original statement, that God is working all things for His own glory. This will be central to our understanding of the covenants of Israel, as well as critical in any understanding of the different economies that God uses to relate to humankind.

Chapter 2
An Outline of History

Change is difficult—difficult to face and often difficult to manage. Few people enjoy it. Children starting school, moving school, or even just changing classes can be unhappy for a while, at least until a new routine has been established. Moving home or starting a new job can be traumatic. Nevertheless, change is also inevitable, change is natural, and change should be expected. Because growth brings change – progress brings change – life brings change. Apart from the immutability of God, nothing stays the same forever. And even the Immutable has initiated change. He has introduced change in His dealings with humankind. The world and its inhabitants are under the sovereign control of God. He is the Creator and all of humankind is responsible to Him. Paul makes this very point in his speech in Athens; *"God, who made the world and everything in it …* *He is Lord of heaven and earth"* (Acts 17:24, emphasis added). Jesus also refers to His Father as *"Lord of heaven and earth"* (Matt. 11:25; see also Luke 10:21, emphasis added). Events that appear to contradict this truth only happen within the permissive will of God. This is clearly the main message of both Job and Daniel. The calamitous events that Satan inflicted on Job and his family were only allowed within the will of God.[10] With this in mind, the Bible sometimes views the world as a household under stewardship. The word used is οἰκονομία so translated in the NASB, *"I have a stewardship entrusted to me"* (1 Cor. 9:17); and *"… if indeed you have heard of the stewardship of God's grace which was given to me for you"* (Eph. 3:2); and again, *"Of this church I was made a minister according to the stewardship from God bestowed on me for your benefit, so that I might fully carry out the preaching of the word of God"* (Col. 1:25). In Ephesians and

Timothy it is translated 'administration.' *"... with a view to an* **administration** *suitable to the fullness of the times, that is, the summing up of all things in Christ, things in the heavens and things on the earth"* (Eph. 1:10, emphasis added); *"and to bring to light what is the* **administration** *of the mystery which for ages has been hidden in God who created all things"* (Eph. 3:9, emphasis added); and Timothy; *"... nor to pay attention to myths and endless genealogies, which give rise to mere speculation rather than furthering the* **administration** *of God which is by faith"* (1 Tim. 1:4, emphasis added). It is not too great a stretch to understand that the world and its occupants are viewed as a household; a household under the sovereign control of the "Lord of heaven and earth;" a household ordered and administered according to the principles He put in place.

In this paradigm, that the world and humanity that occupies it are viewed as a household, it is not an overstatement to say that God has certain 'house' rules. They are the outworking of those principles of righteousness that govern His relationship with humankind. He does not change, He is the Immutable; and He is sovereign and holy. Those that approach Him can only do so by acknowledging this. Celestial servants of His cry night and day, *"Holy, holy, holy, Lord God Almighty"* (Rev. 4:8; cf. Isa. 6:3). But as our circumstances change, so there are changes in God's 'house rules'. It could be considered in terms of growing up. As a child matures so the disciplines placed upon him become more sophisticated. When God changed His house rules, it has usually been in the wake of an event that has had far-reaching effects;

- When Adam transgressed the one commandment, God changed the house rules.
- When the nation Israel was delivered from slavery, for them He changed the house rules.
- When the Messiah died for the sins of the world, He changed the house rules.

In God's household, responsibilities are held by chosen individuals. In the verses where Paul uses the word "οἰκονομία" he refers to his responsibility under God in terms of him occupying the office of steward. In that office and with that responsibility he was charged to promulgate the new "house rules" that were brought in as a result of the sacrifice of the Son of God.

Let us examine the history of the relationship between God and humankind and consider the constancy of the Immutable and the education He instituted for the benefit of us mortals. We will pay particular attention to the change in His "house rules" at the time of the death, resurrection and ascension of the Messiah, and consider how the new house rules were communicated and if the early church found any difficulty in applying them. The covenants of the Bible, the main subject of this book, are statements that illuminate and elucidate God's house rules and an examination of them will surely prove profitable.

Changes initiated by the Immutable

The brackets for the history of humanity on this present earth are the two creations. The record of the first, documented by Moses the historian, is stated simply, *"In the beginning God created the heaven and the earth"* (Gen. 1:1). It is here that human history began. God said, *"Let us make man in our image, after our likeness"* (Gen. 1:26). The Bible also indicates there will be another creation. Peter wrote, *"Nevertheless we, according to His promise, look for **new heavens and a new earth** in which righteousness dwells"* (2 Pet. 3:13, emphasis added). In vision, John saw it. *"Now I saw a **new heaven and a new earth**, for the first heaven and the first earth had passed away"* (Rev. 21:1, emphasis added). Human history on this planet, as we currently know it, will be between the two creations, although eternal life means it will continue forever, albeit under different conditions.

A simple diagram to illustrate:

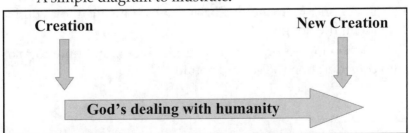

But there are two more major punctuation points needed in the above diagram. One relating to the past and one in connection with the future. The incarnation provided a punctuation mark in past history, an event when *"the Word became flesh and dwelt among us"* (John 1:14).

At the first creation, man was made in God's image (that was at the first punctuation mark), so that at the incarnation God could be made in man's image (that is at the second punctuation mark).

Here is the revised diagram taking into consideration this further information.

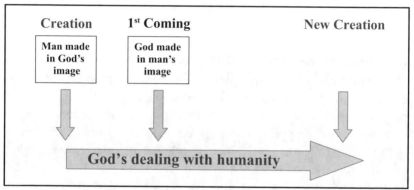

However, the incarnate God, the Messiah, Jesus Christ will visit earth again. The message from on high is, *"This same Jesus, who was taken up from you into heaven, will so come in like manner as you saw Him go into heaven"* (Acts 1:11). He will return to intervene in the affairs of men. First to gather and evacuate from the earth those "in Christ" (both dead and alive); and then shortly after, to rescue the Hebrew nation from annihilation. For those who will be taken to be 'with Christ', they will be remade in the image of Christ,[11] which means they will be remade in the image of God.

So we may modify our diagram again, this time to take into consideration the second coming.

---

11   1 John 3:2

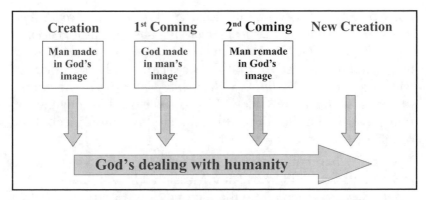

In the period between the first creation and the first coming of Christ, the LORD was mainly occupied in educating humankind in the new house rules, which had been changed because of Adam's disobedience. It is the time that is described in the Bible as the period when God spoke; *"God, who at various times and in various ways spoke in time past to the fathers by the prophets"* (Heb. 1:1). It was a time dominated by prophetic ministry, whether it was a Moses or a Samuel or an Isaiah. It was the period in which the *T'nach*[12] was written; a period that came to a glorious consummation when the Word became flesh and dwelt on earth.[13] The implication is that the *T'nach*, in a sense, was autobiographical because the pre-incarnate Christ spoke through the prophets, and the incarnate Christ stated that they spoke of Himself.[14] The writer of the letter to the Hebrews, who has much to say on the subject, couples the two punctuation points together, that is, the creation and the first coming of Christ; declaring that God *"has in these last days **spoken to us by His Son**, whom He has appointed heir of all things, **through whom also He made the worlds**"* (Heb. 1:2, emphasis added).

The period between the first coming of Christ and His second coming has a different emphasis. It is His present ministry, and it is not so much related to the prophet but to the priest. It

---

12   The Hebrew Scriptures comprising the Torah (the Law), the Nevi'im (the Prophets) and the Kethuvim (the Writings).

13   John 1:14

14   Luke 24:27

is the priestly ministry of intercession. *"Who is he who condemns? It is Christ who died, and furthermore is also risen, who is even at the right hand of God, who also **makes intercession for us**";* (Rom. 8:34, emphasis added) and *"He is also able to save to the uttermost those who come to God through Him, since He always lives **to make intercession for them**"* (Heb. 7:25, emphasis added). He is currently engaged in fulfilling His ministry as a High Priest of the order of Melchizedek.

But when He returns to deal with the crisis affecting the Jewish nation, it will be as King/Messiah. He will deal with the emergency and then judge the nations from His throne. *"When the Son of Man comes in His glory, and all the holy angels with Him, then He will sit on the throne of His glory"* (Matt. 25:31). He will usher in the millennial kingdom, while retaining absolute power. *"He will be great, and will be called the Son of the Highest; and the LORD God will give Him the throne of His father David"* (Luke 1:32). In that millennial kingdom, the apostles will join with Him in reigning over Israel, [15] while the Church will join Him in reigning over the Gentile nations.[16]

Our revised diagram is now:

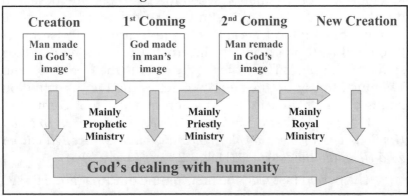

Creation	1st Coming	2nd Coming	New Creation
Man made in God's image	God made in man's image	Man remade in God's image	
	Mainly Prophetic Ministry	Mainly Priestly Ministry	Mainly Royal Ministry

God's dealing with humanity

It is clear from such a diagram, that the rules that govern the household of God must of necessity change, when the ministry of the Son of God changes. Things cannot be the same after the death of Christ, as they were before His death. Things

---

15   Luke 22:30
16   Rev. 5:10

cannot be the same after He has returned as King/Messiah, as they were before that great event.

But our diagram needs further adjustment. It is still a blunt instrument to hold the truth of God's dealings. There are other changes introduced by the Omniscient. We have already noted that Adam's disobedience brought about a change. His existence suffered the greatest change. God had said, *"of the tree of the knowledge of good and evil you shall not eat, for in the day that you eat of it you shall surely die"* (Gen. 2:17). He ate the fruit and paid the penalty, an outcome that had consequences for all his posterity, *"In Adam all die"* (1 Cor. 15:22). In the wake of Adam's transgression, God introduced new "house rules." He could only be approached if the new regimen was recognized, that is, that the wages of sin is death and life is in the grace and gift of God.[17] The death of an animal as a substitute was sufficient to demonstrate acknowledgement of individual failure, remorse for the sinful condition of the penitent, and acceptance of the new regimen. Abel recognized this and brought an acceptable sacrifice. *"Abel ... brought of the firstborn of his flock and of their fat. And the* LORD *respected Abel and his offering"* (Gen. 4:4). The writer of the Hebrew letter identified an essential requirement in the new arrangement – faith. *"**By faith** Abel offered to God a more excellent sacrifice than Cain, through which he obtained witness that he was righteous, God testifying of his gifts"* (Heb. 11:4, emphasis added).

The temptation that was involved in the fall of Adam included the statement from the father of lies, *"You will not surely die"* (Gen. 3:4). But die they did! Genesis chapter five has the refrain for eight of the nine generations listed there, *"and he died"* (Gen. 5:5, 8, 11, 14, 17, 20, 27, 31). And increased wickedness in the world brought about a reinforcement of the principle, *"the wages of sin is death"*. The deluge catastrophically cut short all life upon earth, apart from one family, a family identified as knowing and observing God's 'house rules'. The head of the family was Noah, described as *"a preacher of righteousness"*, in contrast to his contemporaries who are described as *"ungodly"* (2 Pet. 2:5). His experience included the special ingredient

---

17   Cf. Rom. 6:23

"faith;" "*By faith* Noah, being divinely warned of things not yet seen, *moved with godly fear, prepared an ark for the saving of his household, by which he condemned the world and became heir of the righteousness which is according to faith*" (Heb. 11:7, emphasis added).

Regrettably, humanity, infected as it was by the virus of Adam's sin, continued to revolt against the sovereign LORD and united in rebellion against Him. They built a tower for protection from any judgment that could be formed against them. The narrative of the tower of Babel, signifying the rebellion of humankind, is included to identify, among other reasons, how Babylon got its name. It is perhaps, the foundation of the idea that Babylon, in Scripture, always represents the world against God. The unity of these rebellious people was disturbed by the removal of their common language.[18] It is at this point in history that the LORD chose a man to build up an individual relationship, to enter into an arrangement with him, with the promise of large blessings in return for personal commitment. It is here that God's 'house rules' were slightly modified. They were still based on the principle that the wages of sin is death and life is in the grace and gift of God, but here we have an initiative of God that was designed to lead to a solution to the problem of sin. With His eye on a sacrifice that would not simply cover sin but rather cleanse it; He entered into a covenant relationship with Abram, a man He extracted from Babylonia.

---

18   Gen. 11:1-9

Chapter 3
The Abrahamic Covenant

The Abrahamic Covenant was an agreement between the LORD and Abraham, which would have substantial implications for all of humankind. The first expression of the agreement is given early in the *T'nach*, although at that stage it was not called a covenant and Abraham's name was Abram. The arrangement is best described as a promise, although a promise of God, dictated in such clear terms carries all the guarantes of a covenant. *"Now the LORD had said unto Abram, 'Get thee out of thy country, and from thy kindred, and from thy father's house, unto a land that I will shew thee: And I will make of thee a great nation, and I will bless thee, and make thy name great; and thou shalt be a blessing: And I will bless them that bless thee, and curse him that curseth thee: and in thee shall all families of the earth be blessed'"* (Gen. 12:1-3, KJV).

The first and most striking feature of this promise is the use of the word 'bless'. *"I will **bless** you"* and *"I will **bless** those who **bless** you"*. Here is promised the blessing of the LORD that *"makes one rich, And He adds no sorrow with it"* (Prov. 10:22, emphasis added). Not only was blessing promised to Abram, and to those who showed favour to him, but Abram himself was to be a blessing. And not only was the blessing to be of the highest quality, that is, the blessing of the LORD, but it was to be of the widest application, *"in you **all the families of the earth shall be blessed**"*.

The second feature was the assurance that Abram would father a large posterity, *"I will make you **a great nation.**"* Abram was to have children, grandchildren, great-grandchildren, and great-great-grandchildren, and so on.

The third feature was that Abram's election, coupled with personal, national and international blessing, was in the gift of

God, and that the LORD personally committed Himself to keep His promise, *"I will make you a great nation"; "I will bless you and make your name great"; "I will bless those who bless you, and I will curse him who curses you; and in you all the families of the earth shall be blessed."*

The different elements of the promise are, in large part, a reversal of the judgment on Adam. There it was exile, here it is a fellowship (Abraham will be called the friend of God)[19] – there it was pain in childbirth, here it is the joy of children in abundance. In the expansion of the promise into a covenant agreement there will be added a homeland which adds a further contrast because Adam was put out of the most fruitful garden on the planet into a world with uncooperative soil, while Abraham's posterity will live in a land flowing with milk and honey[20]. Like Adam, who had only one command to obey, this promise of great blessing had only one condition, a requirement that Abram leave Ur of the Chaldees, the city "consecrated to the worship of Sin, the Babylonian moon-god".[21] It appears there could be no blessing while Abram remained in Babylonia, the territory that consistently rebelled against the living God.

So Abram had met with God, heard His voice, and been assured of His care. What an encounter! What promises! Stephen, referring to this event said, *"The God of glory[22] appeared to our father Abraham when he was in Mesopotamia, before he dwelt in Haran"* (Acts 7:2, emphasis added).

The Genesis account puts it slightly differently. *"The word of the LORD came to Abram"* (Gen. 15:1) and *"Behold, the word of the LORD came to him"* (Gen.15:4) This is the first mention of the *"word of the LORD"* in the Bible. Stephen identified the *"word of the LORD"* as *"the God of Glory"*. Here, surely, is an indication that it was the pre-incarnate Christ, the Word who was in the

---

19   Jas. 2:23

20   Ex. 3:8,17; 13:5; 33:3; Lev. 20:24; Num. 13:27; 14:8; 16:13-14; Deut. 6:3; 11:9; 26:9,15; 27:3; 31:20; Josh. 5:6; Jer. 11:5; 32:22; Ezek. 20:6,15

21   Easton's Bible Dictionary under the entry "UR".

22   See chapter 1

beginning with God[23], and who is God, that made the covenant with Abram. Jesus, the incarnate glory of God was first the pre-incarnate God of Glory.

Abram did, in fact, leave his home, and followed the guidance of the Lord, albeit, with some delay as he cared for his father. They tarried in Haran, a city also dedicated to the worship of the moon-god, Sin. The fulfillment of the promises of the Lord would have to wait until His chosen vessel had fully departed from the contaminated atmosphere of idolatry. But even when Abram and his household had reached the promised land, Abram's personal commitment yet had some way to run. The severance from his family was still incomplete because his nephew Lot accompanied him. While Lot remained, Abram encountered difficulties. Canaan did not yield its produce to him – it was hit by famine, and he took a detour down into Egypt. If Babylon represents the world against God, Egypt certainly represents the world without God. Alas, Egypt contaminated both Abram[24] and Lot. Lot enjoyed his stay in Egypt, and even after he had left, the land that was watered by the Nile influenced him. When he was required to separate from Abram, he saw an area that reminded him of Egypt.[25] There was a well-watered plain, and cities nearby. With the memory of Egypt fresh in his mind, he chose to pitch his tent towards Sodom. It did not take long for him to relinquish the life of a nomad and become a city dweller – in Sodom, of all places! He not only became a city dweller but an elder of Sodom, sitting in an official capacity at it's gate.[26] Abram, in the meanwhile, continued to look for a *"city which has foundations, whose builder and maker is God"* (Heb. 11:10).

It was not until Lot had gone did God fully confirm the detail of His undertaking. *"And the Lord said to Abram, **after Lot had separated from him**: 'Lift your eyes **now** and look from the place where you are— northward, southward, eastward, and westward; for all the land which you see I give to you and your descendants forever.*

---

23   John 1:1
24   Gen. 16:1 ff
25   Gen. 13:10
26   Gen. 19:1

And I will make your descendants as the dust of the earth; so that if a man could number the dust of the earth, then your descendants also could be numbered. Arise, walk in the land through its length and its width, for I give it to you'" (Gen. 13:14-17, emphasis added). This new word from the LORD, not only re-established the promise of a nation coming from his loins, but also added detail that had not been expressed previously, that is, the land to which he was guided would be given to his descendents, the nation that he would father. It was only after Abram had removed from the influence of both Babylon, and Egypt, and had finally separated from his family, did God repeat the divine promise.

The scriptural assessment of his obedience is summed up in the catalogue of heroes, *"By faith Abraham obeyed when he was called to go out to the place which he would receive as an inheritance. And he went out, not knowing where he was going"* (Heb. 11:8). This verse identifies the element that is at the heart of a covenant relationship with the LORD and an essential ingredient in any obedience offered – faith. *"By faith Abraham obeyed."*

The importance of faith

This element of faith is of vital importance. In a further encounter with God, Abram expressed a prayer for a son; *"LORD GOD, what will You give me, seeing I go childless, and the heir of my house is Eliezer of Damascus?"* (Gen. 15:2). "God replied, *'This one shall not be your heir, but one who will come from your own body shall be your heir.' Then He brought him outside and said, 'Look now toward heaven, and count the stars if you are able to number them.' And He said to him, 'So shall your descendants be'"* (Gen. 15:5) .*"And he believed in the LORD, and He accounted it to him for righteousness"* (Gen. 15:6, emphasis added). This very episode became a cornerstone of the doctrinal writings of Paul, that great expositor of Christology. He referred to it in Romans; *"Abraham believed God, and it was accounted to him for righteousness"* (Rom. 4:3; see also v. 9 and v. 22) and again in his Galatian letter.[27] James also quoted it.[28] It is almost impossible to exag-

---

27   Gal 3:6
28   Jas. 2:23

gerate the magnitude of this episode in the patriarch's life. God made him a promise and he believed. The encounter began with an expression of doubt vocalized by Abram, to which God responded with a renewed promise of staggering proportions, and concluded with Abram fully embracing it. While the fulfillment of the initial covenant depended only on the faithfulness of the LORD, this event, surely known beforehand to God, demonstrated Abram's wholehearted engagement in the purposes of the LORD. Abram's response to the promise, identified faith as the catalyst to activate the blessing that was to come to the Jewish nation, and indeed the blessing that would fall to all who had similar faith to Abram. Those that trust in the promise of God, and in the God of the promise, will be blessed. *"Therefore it is of faith that it might be according to grace, so that the promise might be sure to all the seed, not only to those who are of the law, but also to those who are of the faith of Abraham, who is the father of us all"* (Rom. 4:16). Then Paul wrote after the death of the Messiah, and identified the inclusion of the Gentiles, demonstrates the quality and scope of the covenant with Abram.

The observation of Moses, that Abram believed in the LORD, and He accounted it to him for righteousness, inserted as it is in the historical narrative, must lead to the question, how did Abram demonstrate his faith to make Moses remark on it? And how did the LORD demonstrate He had accepted it and valued it so highly? The answer is found in that which immediately follows. The promise to Abram by the LORD was ratified in such a way to establish it beyond contradiction. It came in the wake of a plea from Abram for such an assurance. When the Lord repeated that Abram would be given future title to the land of Canaan,[29] Abram asked, *"LORD GOD, how shall I know that I will inherit it?"* (Gen. 15:8). The LORD's response was to initiate a ceremony that would give the promise covenant status. This event needs to be laid out in order to get the full impact;

1. God assured Abram that the land would be his. *"I am the LORD, who brought you out of Ur of the Chaldeans, to give you this land to inherit it"* (Gen. 15:7).

---

29   Gen. 15:7

2. Abram asked for some kind of sign to confirm this promise, saying *"LORD GOD, how shall I know that I will inherit it?"* (Gen. 15:8).

3. God commanded Abram to bring an heifer, a goat, a ram and two birds.

4. Abram laid them out in the fashion of a ceremony designed for the ratification of an agreement between two parties; *"Then he brought all these to Him and cut them in two, down the middle, and placed each piece opposite the other; but he did not cut the birds in two"* (Gen. 15:10).

5. These portions of the sacrifice had to be protected by Abram; *"And when the vultures came down on the carcasses, Abram drove them away"* (Gen. 15:11).

6. After the sun went down, God placed Abram in a deep sleep during which he had a nightmarish dream. *"Now when the sun was going down, a deep sleep fell upon Abram; and behold, horror and great darkness fell upon him"* (Gen. 15:12).

7. Then God spoke to Abram and told him the time for possessing the land was not yet, so they would not occupy the land for almost more than half a millennia. *"Know certainly that your descendants will be strangers in a land that is not theirs, and will serve them, and they will afflict them four hundred years. And also the nation whom they serve I will judge; afterward they shall come out with great possessions"* (Gen. 15:13-14). [30]

8. God indicated that Abram would have long life. *"Now as for you, you shall go to your fathers in peace; you shall be buried at a good old age"* (Gen. 15:15).

---

[30] Maimonides (Moses Ben Maimon), the celebrated Jewish commentator from the 12th century, suggests the oppression of Israel in Egypt was the result of Abram's inadvertent sin in going down to Egypt at the time of famine in Canaan. (See his comment on Gen. 12:10 referred to in the Jewish Study Bible.)

9. God added the reason for the delay in their taking possession of the land. *"But in the fourth generation they shall return here, for the iniquity of the Amorites is not yet complete"* (Gen. 15:16). This meant that the Amorites, one of the occupying tribes of Canaan were not yet ripe for punishment - punishment here being the loss of Canaan.

10. In the darkness of an eastern night after the sun had set, Abram's deep sleep continued, in which God unilaterally established the covenant between the two of them. *"And it came to pass, when the sun went down and it was dark, that behold, there appeared a smoking oven and a burning torch that passed between those pieces. On the same day the LORD made a covenant with Abram, saying: 'To your descendants I have given this land, from the river of Egypt to the great river, the River Euphrates— the Kenites, the Kenezzites, the Kadmonites, the Hittites, the Perizzites, the Rephaim, the Amorites, the Canaanites, the Girgashites, and the Jebusites'"* (Gen. 15:17-21).

The fire of the theophany, for such it was, symbolized judgment on the enemies of the seed of Abram, who were the subject of the prophecy that introduced the event. From the furnace there emanated shafts of fire. While the contract was made between the two parties, it is clear that the LORD was the only guarantor of the contract, a covenant of grant. He alone passed between the separated animal carcasses. Abram was present solely as the beneficiary.

But how was the promised blessing of God to be realized? Sarai was barren – she had not, nor could have, children. The answer seemed obvious - Abram must take another wife. Sarai's maid, Hagar, brought up from Egypt, was chosen. But God's ways are higher than man's ways, even Abram's. As Abram could not be blessed while resident in Babylonia, so also an Egyptian slave girl cannot be the mother of the nation elected by God to be the cradle that would hold the Messiah. Ishmael was born and Ishmael would be the father of a great nation, but it would not be the elect people.[31]

The covenant confirmed

At ninety-nine years of age, fourteen years after the covenant had been made, God again appeared to Abram, and said, *"I am Almighty God; walk before Me and be blameless. And I will make My covenant between Me and you, and will multiply you exceedingly"* (Gen. 17:1-3). Here is the first time in the Bible that the name *"El Shaddai"* (God Almighty or God All-sufficient) is used. *'El'* is God, singular. It signifies strong or first, and identifies Him as the first great cause. The etymology of *'Shaddai'* is less clear. Two aspects seem to have preference. One, that it is the combination of two elements, *'Sha'* (the one who) and *'dai'* (is sufficient). This is sometimes preferred because *'shad'* means breast, and can refer to the God who feeds and nourishes. He is the God who is all sufficient. Alternatively, it may come from *'shadad'* which refers to His power and might. The translators usually adopt this meaning and translate *'El Shaddai'* with the title 'God Almighty'. Either way, it is a name that describes the covenant God, as possessing the power to fulfill His promise, even when nature itself is powerless to secure it. The Name by which the Lord introduced Himself was to bring assurance to Abram that though he was past age for fathering a child, and Sarai was barren, nevertheless an innumerable posterity would be his. With this in mind the Lord encouraged Abram to pursue a walk before Him that would be blameless.

The revelation of Abram's new Name was followed immediately by the declaration that the time had come for the fulfillment of the covenant; *"And I will make My covenant between Me and you, and will multiply you exceedingly"* (Gen. 17:2). This does not signify a new covenant but the beginning of the execution of the previously agreed contract. God set in motion that which was needed for the implementation of His pledge. Abram was overwhelmed and prostrated himself before the Lord. The Lord continued, *"As for Me, behold, My covenant is with you, and you*

---

31   Gal. 4:21-31

shall be a father of many nations. No longer shall your name be called Abram, but your name shall be Abraham; for I have made you a father of many nations. I will make you exceedingly fruitful; and I will make nations of you, and kings shall come from you" (Gen. 17:4-6).

"As for Me", that is, on My part,

1. *"I will establish My covenant between Me and you and your descendants after you in their generations, for an **everlasting covenant**, to be God to you and your descendants after you"* (Gen. 17:7, emphasis added). The eternal God established an eternal covenant with Abram and his posterity. God is pleased to be known as the God of Abraham.[32] He is the God of Abraham and the God of Israel. *"I will be their God"* (v. 8).

2. *"You shall be a father of many nations."* This covenant gets better and better. Not simply the father of *"a great nation"*, but now *"a father of many nations"*. Abram was to be the ancestor of nations and kings (v.6). To a man whose body was dead,[33] God said he would be *"exceedingly fruitful"*. God had said to Adam, *"Be fruitful and multiply; fill the earth"* (Gen 1:28). Alas, in Adam all die, but in Abram's seed all live.[34]

3. *"Also I give to you and your descendants after you the land in which you are a stranger, all the land of Canaan, as an everlasting possession; and I will be their God"* (Gen. 17:8). The land to which he had been led was given to him and his descendents, for an *"everlasting possession"* repeating the truth that the Abrahamic covenant is eternal. The *"I give"* indicates it is unconditional.

Moreover, the extent of the covenant relationship between Abram and the LORD was to be fully advertised to all peoples

---

32   Gen. 26:24; 28:13; Ex. 3:6; 3:15, 16; 4:5; cf. Gen. 31:42; 31:53; 1 Kgs. 18:36; 1 Chron. 29:18; 2 Chron. 30:6; Ps. 47:9; Matt. 22:32; Mark 12:26; Luke 20:37; Acts 3:13; Acts 7:32

33   Rom. 4:19

34   1 Cor. 15:22

because it would forever be incorporated into his name, which God changed from Abram (high father) into Abraham (father of a multitude). Under God, he was to be a father of many nations.

To come under the Abrahamic covenant each individual Jewish male had to be circumcised.[35] Moreover, the covenant was to come through a son of promise. *"And God said unto Abraham, As for Sarai thy wife, thou shalt not call her name Sarai, but Sarah shall her name be. And I will bless her, and give thee a son also of her: yea, I will bless her, and she shall be a mother of nations; kings of people shall be of her"* (Gen. 17:15,16, KVG). At this Abram, now Abraham, laughed. He was one hundred years old, and Sarah was ninety. "Not that he either ridiculed the promise of God, or treated it as a fable, or rejected it altogether; but, as often happens when things occur which are least expected, partly lifted up with joy, partly carried out of himself with wonder, he burst out into laughter"(Calvin).[36] "The promise was so immensely great, that he sank in adoration to the ground, and so immensely paradoxical, that he could not help laughing" (Delitzsch).[37] At this point Abraham reminded the Omniscient that he had already taken steps to help the Omnipotent fulfill His promise. He had a son, Ishmael. The LORD declared that Ishmael would become a great nation, but the covenant would be through the son that Sarah would bear, named Isaac. Embracing fully the covenant, Abraham had all the males in his household circumcised.

Leaving no stone unturned, God visited Abraham, who was now in full covenant relationship with Him, having been circumcised along with his household. The LORD (so identified in Gen. 18:13) along with two angels, called on Abraham and Sarah to strengthen Sarah's faith for the birth of a son. The three, in human form, shared a meal with Abraham during which they asked for Sarah. She, standing within earshot, was permit-

---

35 Gen. 17:10-14

36 Quoted by Keil, C. F., & Delitzsch, F., <u>Commentary on the Old Testament</u>. (1:144). (Peabody, MA: Hendrickson, 2002)

37 In Keil, C. F., & Delitzsch, F., <u>Commentary on the Old Testament</u>. (1:144). (Peabody, MA: Hendrickson, 2002)

ted to overhear the conversation in which the LORD unveiled the timetable for the birth of Isaac. Within a year, Sarah would be a mother. Sarah laughed and was reproved. Nevertheless, her faith was strengthened, and the Scriptures record, *"By faith Sarah herself also received strength to conceive seed, and she bore a child when she was past the age, because she judged Him faithful who had promised"* (Heb. 11:11). Behold, the grace of God, in that He paid her a personal visit to encourage her faith in Him. He asked, *"Is anything too hard for the LORD?"* and promised, *"At the appointed time I will return to you, according to the time of life, and Sarah shall have a son"* (Gen. 18:14). So Sarah had a boy just as the LORD had said, when Abraham was a hundred years old. They called him Isaac (a play on the word 'laughter').

The Covenant again Confirmed

Any biography of Abraham will demonstrate the importance of the event recorded in Genesis chapter 22, known as the *"Akedah"* or "binding". The LORD asked Abraham to sacrifice Isaac, the son of promise, on an altar on Mount Moriah. This he was prepared to do, but was finally restrained by a word from the LORD. Instead, he offered a ram, which was providentially available, as a substitute for Isaac. This sacrifice of an animal in place of the firstborn son will take on much larger proportions in Exodus at the redemption of the nation.

A second word from the LORD at this time, given as a result of the *"Akedah"*, reiterated the former covenant promises. *"By Myself I have sworn, says the LORD, because you have done this thing, and have not withheld your son, your only son— blessing I will bless you, and multiplying I will multiply your descendants as the stars of the heaven and as the sand which is on the seashore; and your descendants shall possess the gate of their enemies. In your seed all the nations of the earth shall be blessed, because you have obeyed My voice"* (Gen. 22:16-18).

To confirm the immutability of this covenant, the LORD re-established it with an oath, and because He could swear by no greater,[38] He used His own Name to support the vow. While this is the only time He used an oath with the Patriarchs, they often returned to this confirming of the covenant, to find encouragement and strength. Indeed the Lord Himself returned to this encounter to encourage them. As an example of the first, when Abraham needed to find a wife for Isaac for the progeny to continue, it is this episode he remembers when commissioning his senior steward to search for a suitable bride.[39] In respect of the second, the Lord referred to it when requiring Isaac to stay clear of Egypt, despite a famine in the land,[40] and when He gave instructions to Moses at the time of the Exodus from Egypt.[41] Joseph referred to it when making provision for his remains to be taken to Canaan.[42] Indeed, David expanded this oath to support the Davidic Covenant.[43]

Summary So Far

In Genesis chapter twelve, God elected a man, Abram, and called him out of the Babylonian city of Ur, separating him from idolatry and rebellious influences. God promised personal, national and international blessing. The blessing was to be in several areas: (i) his posterity was to be a great nation, (ii) they would be the catalyst for blessing, and (iii) they would possess a particular geographic area, a land.

Further affirmations of the covenant
Issac and the Covenant

The Lord had clearly indicated that the fulfillment of the covenant was to be through Isaac, although Abraham had other sons (six with Keturah[44], as well as Hagar's son Ishmael). Therefore, it was appropriate that Isaac should be assured of

---

38   Heb. 6:13
39   Gen. 24:1 ff (see particularly v.7)
40   Gen. 26:1 ff (see particularly v.3)
41   Ex. 13:1 ff (see particularly vv.5 & 11) See also Ex. 33:1
42   Gen. 50:24-25
43   Ps. 89:36; Ps. 132:11
44   Gen. 25:1-2

the performance of the promise. The occasion was another famine in Canaan. God appeared to Isaac to instruct him not to make the same mistake as his father, and go down to Egypt, but rather stay in the Promised Land. *"Dwell in this land, and I will be with you and bless you; for to you and your descendants I give all these lands, and I will perform the oath which I swore to Abraham your father. And I will make your descendants multiply as the stars of heaven; I will give to your descendants all these lands; and in your seed all the nations of the earth shall be blessed"* (Gen. 26:4). Isaac stayed and enjoyed immediate blessing. His flocks and herds increased substantially and he enlarged the number of servants in his household to cope with the extra work that the increased wealth generated. He became the envy of the inhabitants of the land. This jealousy led to conflict, but God revisited him and assured him of His protection, while reminding him of the covenant, *"I am the God of your father Abraham; do not fear, for I am with you. I will bless you and multiply your descendants for My servant Abraham's sake"* (Gen. 26:24). This was at Beersheba, a location where Abraham had previously stayed, and the location that Jacob would inhabit after him.

The covenant was to continue through the generations, but Isaac had two sons, twins, Esau and Jacob. Through which of these should it persist? Rebecca's confinement was difficult— the twins struggled in her womb. The distress caused her to cry, *"Why am I like this?"* (Gen. 25:22). In response to her enquiry the LORD made her aware of a continuing struggle between the posterity of the two boys, when the younger would obtain precedence over the elder. The younger was, of course, Jacob who grasped the heel of his brother, an accident of birth that provided his name. The disposition of the developing children was in sharp contrast in that Esau was an outdoor man, a hunter, whereas Jacob found pleasure in the activities of the home. In consequence, Esau was the favorite of Isaac while Jacob was the favorite of Rebecca. As they grew, so the contrast became more evident, and an incident is recorded that delineates the unmistakable difference between them. Esau, returning from the hunt and famished, called for some of the food that Jacob was cooking. The younger twin, taking an opportunity to get the best of his brother, required an exorbitant price for the meal—the first-born's birthright. This included not only the double portion of the inheritance, but also, because of their position in the ancestral line, the position of tribal chief, which in turn, incorporated the rule over the whole of the family,[45] not just his own children. Jacob certainly knew the birthright was important, but whether he knew its full value is uncertain. That it would extend to the blessing incorporated in the covenant, and the future possession of Canaan, became clearer later.[46] What was clear—Esau was not a spiritual man, (the writer to Hebrew Christians labeled him a 'profane' person)[47] and thought he was getting the best of Jacob, inasmuch as the payment was simply a promise – and, in his view, a promise of little value at that!

In the course of time, Isaac, with diminishing sight and reducing natural vigor, decided it was time to bless his sons. Even if he knew of the prophetic word given to Rebekah indicating that the elder would serve the younger, he did not consider it should influence his action in giving Esau the blessing of the firstborn. After all, Esau is not only his firstborn but also his pride and joy. But Rebekah would not see Jacob overlooked at this time and with a mixture of domestic skill and deception, obtained for Jacob the premier blessing. Isaac, in the elevated state of mind of the inspired poet said:

"Surely, the smell of my son
Is like the smell of a field
Which the LORD has blessed.
Therefore may God give you
Of the dew of heaven,
Of the fatness of the earth,
And plenty of grain and wine.
Let peoples serve you,
And nations bow down to you.

---

45   Gen. 27:29
46   Gen. 27:4; 27-29; 28:4
47   Heb. 12:16

Be master over your brethren,
And let your mother's sons bow down to you.
Cursed be everyone who curses you,
And blessed be those who bless you!" (Gen. 27:27-29).

Thus, the sovereign purposes of God, pronounced in the Abrahamic covenant, came to the fore in the blessing of Jacob by Isaac. While Isaac is unable to rise to the heights of the original covenant, as seen by his use of Elohim as the name of God in blessing, nevertheless many of the ingredients of the covenant are presented here. The land that he was to occupy would be a land blessed by the Lord, a land of plenty. And his language clearly rose to include Jacob's posterity who would be the touchstone for blessing for all nations. Those that blessed Jacob and his issue would themselves be blessed, and those that cursed him and his issue would themselves be cursed. In such an unpromising family situation did the promise of blessing pass to Abraham's grandson Jacob.

Jacob and the Covenant

As Isaac was assured of the promise of blessing, so also was Jacob. It took place when he traveled toward Haran to find a wife from within Rebekah's family circle. He had his first direct encounter with God. In a dream he saw heaven and earth in communication via a ladder, suggesting communication between the God of heaven and his people on earth. Above, in heaven, the LORD stood and to the lonely, weary, traveler pledged a complete fulfillment of all the promises made to his forefathers, and assured him of protection on his journey and a safe return to his home. *"I am the LORD God of Abraham your father and the God of Isaac; the land on which you lie I will give to you and your descendants. Also your descendants shall be as the dust of the earth; you shall spread abroad to the west and the east, to the north and the south; and in you and in your seed all the families of the earth shall be blessed. Behold, I am with you and will keep you wherever you go, and will bring you back to this land,"*(Gen.28.13-15) adding, *"I will not leave you until I have done what I have spoken to you."*

45

For those who were to be the founders of a nation with an agricultural economy, it is entirely appropriate that the promises were encapsulated in 'land', 'seed' and 'blessing'. The 'land' element in the covenant naturally comes first, followed by the 'seed' that was to be planted in the land, together with the assurance of God's 'blessing' on the crop. As with a natural crop, the seed would multiply exceedingly. Furthermore, the blessing on the seed of Jacob would extend to all areas of the globe as the posterity of Jacob spread west and east, north and south, and touch all of humankind. Nevertheless, the land on which he lay would be their ultimate home, for to that land would they return. Thus the blessing, passed to Jacob from Isaac his father, and which was the direct cause of him leaving home, is confirmed by the only One who could bring it to pass, the author of the blessing Himself, the LORD. Ah! The condescension of God!

While it was required that Isaac remain in the land, there came a time when Jacob was given permission to leave the land. The foundation of the nation was already laid in that he had twelve sons, and the process was to begin, in which they would grow into a great nation. The elevation of Jacob's son Joseph in Egypt prepared the way for the removal of Jacob's (now renamed Israel's) family from Canaan, a land in which they had title but not yet possession. Judah's alliance with the Canaanites[48] demonstrated how vulnerable they were as a family, to the pressures of living in a land where their separation could easily be compromised, and their divine call could be endangered. The LORD authorized their temporary removal from the land, and Joseph's promotion provided the perfect means and motivation for the seed to be transplanted in Egyptian soil. Nevertheless, the events that brought about their move must have brought disquiet to the mind of Jacob. At such a time, and in such circumstances, God spoke a word of encouragement to him. He said, *"I am God, the God of your father; do not fear to go down to Egypt, for **I will make of you a great nation there**. I will go down with you to Egypt, and I will also surely bring you up again; and Joseph will put his hand on your eyes"* (Gen. 46:3-4). And here

---

48   Gen. 38

we have come, as it were, full circle, returning to God's dealing with Abram, when He said, *"Know certainly that your descendants will be strangers in a land that is not theirs, and will serve them, and they will afflict them four hundred years. And also the nation whom they serve I will judge; afterward they shall come out with great possessions. ...But in the fourth generation they shall return here, for the iniquity of the Amorites is not yet complete"* (Gen. 15:13-16).

The Abrahamic Covenant summarized

The terms of the Abrahamic covenant indicate it is the basis of the dealings of the LORD with the Jewish nation, and through them, with the rest of humankind. Here is a summary of the provisions of the covenant.

1. Abram was to be father of a great nation (Gen. 12:2; 13:16; 15:5; 17:1-2; 17:7; 22:17).

2. This nation would possess the land of Canaan (Gen.12:7; 13:14-15; 13:17; 15:17-21; 17:8).

3. He himself would enjoy the blessing of the LORD (Gen. 12:2; 24:1).

4. Abram's name would be great (Gen. 12:2); changed later to Abraham (Gen. 17:5).

5. He would be a blessing to others (Gen. 12:2); indeed the blessing would extend to nations, peoples and families (Gen. 12:3; 22:18).

6. Those who blessed Abram (and his seed) would be blessed; those who cursed Abram (and his seed) would be cursed (Gen. 12:2; 22:15-18; 26:3; 26:24; 27:29; 28:4).

7. Abraham would father more than one nation (Gen. 17:4-6).

The covenant was to be an everlasting covenant between God and Abraham, and Abraham's posterity,[49] through Isaacb

---

49   Gen. 17:7-8

(Sarah's son)[50] and Jacob[51]. The sign of the covenant was to be circumcision.[52]

Returning to our diagrammatic outline, the Abrahamic covenant begins very near to the first downward arrow, the creation of Adam (Abraham is introduced into Scripture at the end of chapter 11 of the book of Genesis), and continues in effect for the whole historical length of the diagram, thus:

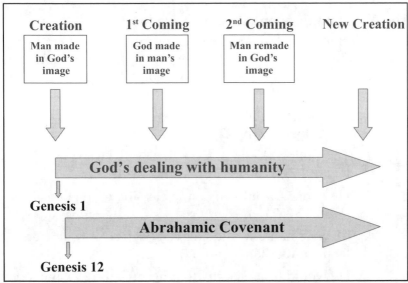

From the foregoing, it is clear that the importance of the Abrahamic covenant cannot be exaggerated.

---

50   Gen. 17:15-16; 18:14; 26:4
51   Gen. 25:23
52   Gen. 17:10-14

Chapter 4
The Abrahamic Covenant –
Its Purpose and Effect

Even before the foundation of the world God had been working to a plan. Essentially it was two fold. It was to produce a being that He could have fellowship with – that would learn from His wisdom and respond to His love. It would be an organism made up of those that already bore His imprint, that is, those that were made in His image and likeness, and so could be in perfect harmony with His own nature and would be able to be loved by Him, and love Him in return. In His wisdom and with His foresight He had already discounted the possibility of one individual member of His creation being able to fill this requirement. The disappointment, for disappointment it must have been, of the fall of Lucifer, suggests that this decision was the correct one, although He has given us no information to suggest that Lucifer or any of the angelic host were ever capable of responding to His love in any meaningful way. They were created as His servants to serve Him, although the nature of the Godhead demanded that even the service of such beings should be a willing service and not by compulsion. In consequence they were given the freedom of choice. No! The Omniscient One embarked on a course of action that would result in an organic, living entity that would be capable of fellowship with the Godhead by reason of many individual parts, each bringing something unique and special to the relationship. And that by reason of great numbers and a wide array of gifts and abilities, harnessed together by a corporate delight in fellowship with God, they would collectively provide a beating heart of love that could respond to their divine Creator. His revealed aim then, is to have a great celestial ceremony amidst great rejoicing and in front of a great cloud of witnesses, to enter into a covenant relationship with the members of this foreknown and predestined group, who, although disparate in themselves are bound to each other by a common love of the Godhead. They will, when it takes place, be a united group, 'all one in Christ Jesus'. The marriage ceremony between the Son of God and the Church is one of the last scenes provided for us in Scripture.

But such an ambition would require a member of the Godhead to forge a link between Himself and humankind. Moreover, the great gift of moral freedom, which would be an essential element in this union, would ultimately produce a need for a plan of salvation, because the foreknowledge and wisdom of God could predict the sin of Adam and the wide ranging consequence of his fall. The member of the Godhead entrusted with this task was the Son, who would be incarnate in the person of Jesus of Nazareth. His eternal position within the structure of the Godhead together with the briefest outline of the great master plan can be discovered within His prayer to God the Father, the night before He was crucified. He said, *"Father, I desire that they also whom You gave Me may be with Me where I am, that they may behold My glory which You have given Me; for You loved Me before the foundation of the world"* (John 17:24). His existence and His relationship with the Father before the beginning of time is the basis for the request. It also reveals that there is to be a relationship with the redeemed in the future, because His prayer was not only for His immediate friends and followers but also for those who would later become His followers,[53] and be identified by the collective noun 'Church' for this also was foreknown and incorporated into God's great purpose before the beginning of time. They were chosen, *"in Him before the foundation of the world, that* (they) *should be holy and without blame before Him in love"* (Eph. 1:4). Peter is the one who describes the incredible means of grace that would enable this magnificent gesture of love; *"You were not redeemed with corruptible things, like silver or gold ...but with the precious blood of Christ, as of a lamb without blemish and without spot. He indeed was foreordained before*

---

53   John 17:20

the foundation of the world, but was manifest in these last times for you" (1 Pet. 1:18-20).

That there was such a program in place is revealed in the prophecy uttered at the fall of Adam. Satan, the arch enemy of God who master-minded the sin of Adam, was told in respect of the seed of the woman, *"He shall bruise your head"*, adding that it would be at some personal cost, *"And you shall bruise His heel"* (Gen. 3:15). These mysterious words need history to explain them, but now it is clear they refer to the defeat of Satan at Calvary.

But our purpose here is to consider how the Abrahamic Covenant fits into this overall purpose of God. Here are some suggestions.

1. The whole scheme of things will rest on an incarnation. The wisdom of God created man in His image, and the purpose of God provided for the creation of the Church. Therefore it would seem essential that God should be created in man's image, to enjoy this meaningful relationship. In other words, man was created in God's image, so that God could be created in man's image, so that man could be re-created in God's image and in a unity named 'Church' be called to join the Son of God in marriage.

2. Since the Godhead exists in the eternal state, the incarnation would also be needed to accomplish a redemption that would result in mortals putting on immortality. For this union to work, the members of the 'Church' need to live for ever.

3. Abraham was chosen to father a nation that could accommodate the incarnation.

4. Identifying a particular nation at its beginning, that is, in the loins of one man, was necessary because this particular nation will have to provide the conditions that would allow the Son of God to live a holy life essentially without persecution or opposition. With Abraham God began with an almost blank canvas.

5. The nation would have to be trained in such a way that the redemptive plan of God could be accomplished seamlessly within its religious structure.

6. The nation would have to be brought into a relationship with the Godhead that would signify that God was prepared to be related to humankind. (Israel is first called 'the first-born' of God, then later the 'wife' of Jehovah).

7. Once redemption was accomplished the nation could provide a focal point for the offer of a relationship with God to be advertised. It would provide fertile ground for the gospel to take root and flourish.

8. Moreover, a nation that had been separated by its training and its relationship to the LORD, when scattered among the nations, as they surely would be, would be the best advertisement for the truth of monotheism. The God of Abraham and the God of Israel would be known in all lands.

So God selected a man, Abram, tested him and found him strong in faith, and suitable to be father of such a nation – more than that – he would be suitable to be the father of many nations, and the father of the faithful. This is the man he trained and entered into a covenant relationship with. So the line of the seed of the woman is going to come through Abraham, Isaac and Israel. The Son of God must come from this nation.

CHAPTER 5

The Mosaic Covenant

From such small beginnings, the purposes of God grew. There was no great sweeping movement of the Spirit of God at that time, just the Omnipotent dealing with one man. From this individual Abram, and his wife Sarai, was to be brought a nation whose number could not be counted. It did not matter that Sarai was barren or that Abram was allowed to grow old, God's promise would hold. And not only was the LORD prepared to deal with just one man, but was prepared to let him proceed at his own pace. Oh! The grace of God. But thereafter the pace quickened. Not only was a nation to be produced from Abraham, as his new name indicated, but it would now be done with some urgency. "Be fruitful", is the command of the LORD. In the same way as He commanded Adam and Eve, and later Noah, to "be fruitful"; He commanded Jacob "be fruitful". And for the family to grow into a nation, that would be without number (as the stars of heaven, the dust of the earth or the sand on the seashore) the seed would need to be planted in fertile soil, where it would bear fruit a hundredfold. Furthermore, not only were they to be innumerable but also separate, that is, holy unto the LORD.

The LORD had already indicated to Abraham that the land in which they would dwell was to be Canaan. This was not some territory picked at random, but a strategically placed geographical location. It was the crossroads where the three main streams of humanity meet. It was the junction of the three main continents, Asia, Africa and Europe; those territories where the sons of Noah settled; Shem in Asia, Ham in Africa, and Japheth in Europe. Therefore, the soil for the incubation of the seed of Abraham had to be within a reasonable distance of Canaan.

The solution was to plant the seed in the hothouse climate of Egypt. In preparation for the move of Jacob's family to Egypt, the LORD incorporated into His plan the actions of Jacob's sons when they sold their brother into slavery. Joseph referred to it when he was reunited with his family. He said, *"God sent me before you to preserve a posterity for you in the earth"* (Gen. 45:7). Thus, the plan of God became evident, for there they would know protection (the protection of Joseph to begin with; and afterward the dynasty that Joseph served). There they could multiply while remaining separate. They would not be absorbed because their separation would be both physical and cultural. Physical, because they would live in a region apart from the main population – that of Goshen; and cultural, because shepherds and sheep farming were tolerated but not embraced by the Egyptian population. However, Egypt could not be their home – they would have to be transplanted in Canaan. But how would you get the new-born nation to leave Egypt? And when they left, they all had to leave – none to remain. So how would you get a nation of more than two million people to leave Egypt of their own accord? Alas, you could not. The only way to extract them from their life in Goshen was to get the Egyptians to drive them out, and the only way the Egyptians would drive them out, is if they became totally odious to them. Such was the background to the nation's Egyptian bondage and their exodus. This does not imply that the LORD orchestrated the period of oppression, only that, in his wisdom, He was able to predict and incorporate the actions of the Egyptian leadership into His plans for the infant nation. His ways are higher than our ways.[54]

Before they could enjoy liberty away from Egypt there would be commands to be obeyed, blood to be shed, and claims to be met. The final break from the oppressive regime came because they obeyed the commands, shed the blood and acknowledged God's claims. The requirements imposed on Israelite households at the time they began their escape from their Egyptian prison, are given in Exodus chapter twelve. God's instructions through Moses were very particular. Each household was to kill, roast and eat a lamb or kid as their last meal

---

54   Isa. 55.8: 9

in Egypt.[55] The animal had to be a male, one year old, in good health, with no visible defects – only a healthy animal would be suitable as a sacrifice to the LORD and only such an animal could be the substitute for someone who was to be consecrated to God.[56] Though they did not know it at the time, only such an animal could foreshadow the Messiah, the true Lamb of God, who is holy, harmless, undefiled and separate from sinners.[57]

The animal, chosen on the 10th of the month Abib or Nisan as it was later known,[58] was to be slain on the 14th. The head of each household was to slay the lamb at twilight.[59] These men would occupy the office of priest, and thereby constitute Israel as a nation of priests. The concept 'kingdom of priests' would be a foundational aspect of the covenant between the LORD and Israel that would be agreed at Mount Sinai.[60] They were to daub the blood of the animal on the door surround, as evidence that the household had obeyed God's instructions and fulfilled the necessary conditions for salvation. Then, when God visited Egypt with judgment, the blood of the substitute protected the Israelite homes, while Egyptian homes, that had no such protection, suffered the death of their firstborn. The Hebrew word for Passover (Pesach) comes from a verb meaning 'to pass over', and clearly refers to the means by which they escaped the judgment that fell on Egypt.[61] They were to eat the meal dressed for their journey, and be prepared to leave at a moment's notice.

Their deliverance was so momentous that the calendar was re-ordered. *"This month shall be your beginning of months; it shall be the first month of the year to you"* (Ex. 12:2). Their religious year was to begin with the month of *Abib*. Under the general name of 'Passover', this festival was incorporated into the life of the nation as a great educational tool in the hands of the

---

55   Ex. 12:1-13
56   Ex. 13:2
57   Heb. 7:26
58   Its Babylonian name (Neh. 2:1; Est. 3:7)
59   Ex. 12:6
60   Ex. 19:6
61   Ex. 12:13; 27

LORD. It would be the first event of their religious year.[62] This festival, that immortalized the birth of the nation, established for all future generations, the principles of substitution and consecration. And in light of the loss of the firstborn of Egypt and the deliverance of the firstborn of Israel, God claimed Israel's firstborn for His own. Thus, the Egyptian Passover began the process of making Israel a unique and separate nation. A key feature of the ordering of the festival was that only those covered by the **Abrahamic** covenant could be admitted to the Passover meal.[63]

In addition to the re-ordering of the calendar, the LORD memorialized the deliverance of the nation with a festival, *"Speak to the children of Israel, and say to them ...these are My feasts. On the fourteenth day of the first month at twilight is the LORD's Passover"*, (Lev.23.2,5) a festival that was to commemorate Israel's birth as a nation, and celebrate their subsequent new life in His care. And as birth is followed by growth, so the nation would grow in the knowledge of Him and His purposes. In practical terms, separation from Egypt was to be followed by a separation to God. A consecrated walk with the LORD, in an ever increasing understanding of His character and will, was to be the process, and a covenant between the LORD and Israel would set out details of the behavior expected of the nation chosen by God to be His special treasure.

The Giving of the Law was for Israel, God's new 'house rules'

Since the nation's period of slavery had left them ill-prepared for nationhood, God set about providing them with leadership—a moral and ethical code by which to live—and government that would produce discipline and order. The nation was to be ordered as a theocracy so the code by which they were to be molded would be issued from the throne of heaven. These regulations were to be His house-rules. They would not be an end in themselves – they would be preparatory for a further outworking of the purposes of their divine Author. Moses was

---

62   Exod. 12:14
63   Exod. 12:47-48

called into the presence of God, where an offer of a covenant was made; *"And Moses went up to God, and the* Lord *called to him from the mountain, saying, 'Thus you shall say to the house of Jacob, and tell the children of Israel: 'You have seen what I did to the Egyptians, and how I bore you on eagles' wings and brought you to Myself.' Now therefore, if you will indeed obey My voice and keep My covenant, then you shall be a special treasure to Me above all people; for all the earth is Mine. And you shall be to Me a kingdom of priests and a holy nation.'"* (Ex. 19:3-6) To this offer they unanimously replied, *"All that the* Lord *has spoken we will do"* (Ex. 19:8).

But it would be necessary for every individual Israelite to understand that these regulations were authored by the Lord and not by Moses. Therefore the initial communication of the house-rules would be by direct communication from above. The Decalogue on which the Law was to be based would first be audibly communicated by God Himself, then written with His finger on tablets of stone while attended by some of nature's most awesome and violent events. The unfolding drama that was the offering of the covenant took place on and around Mount Sinai, and more than two million witnessed it. Thunders, lightening and earthquakes attended the descent of the Lord on to the pinnacle of Horeb. With such evident manifestations of the presence and mind of God, everyone was clear about one thing - this code was to be non-negotiable – there would be no modifying of its requirements: either obey it, or face the Omnipotent and explain why!

The code under which they would serve would teach them to differentiate between holy and unholy, between clean and unclean. Since the issuing of the code coincided with the time of the nation's liberation from slavery, and it might appear to the uninitiated that they exchanged one form of slavery for another - they were now to be under the bondage of the Law. But these regulations were accompanied by great and majestic promises of blessing and peace and happiness. Only by submitting to theocratic rule from above could they know true freedom and prosperity. As Matheson wrote, "make me a captive,

Lord, and then I shall be free".[64]

So Israel, from the dark womb of Egypt, was brought to birth as a nation, and called the firstborn of the Lord. *"Thus says the Lord: 'Israel is My son, My firstborn'"* (Ex. 4:22). Here, it is clear that the Mosaic covenant was established between Israel and the Lord. No other nations are involved, no other combination of peoples are involved. Moses repeats this truth, when he addresses the nation at the end of his life; *"For what great nation is there that has God so near to it, as the Lord our God is to us, for whatever reason we may call upon Him? And what great nation is there that has such statutes and righteous judgments as are in all this law which I set before you this day?"* (Deut. 4:7-8). This is repeated in the 'writings'; *"He declares His word to Jacob, His statutes and His judgments to Israel. He has not dealt thus with any nation; And as for His judgments, they have not known them. Praise the Lord!"* (Ps. 147:19-20) and the prophets, *"Remember the Law of Moses, My servant, Which I commanded him in Horeb for all Israel, With the statutes and judgments"* (Mal. 4:4).

The terms of the Mosaic Covenant have been examined and analyzed over centuries, and Jewish legal experts have ordered and codified it in such a way that the nation could understand its requirements and obey its precepts. R. Simlai, a Palestinian haggadist, summarized their conclusion; "Six hundred and thirteen commandments were revealed to Moses; 365 being prohibitions equal in number to the days of the year, and 248 being mandates corresponding in number to the bones of the human body."[65] The number 613 is found as early as tannaitic times—e.g., in a saying of Simon ben Eleazar and one of Simon ben Azzai—and is apparently based upon ancient tradition.[66] The need to understand and obey it arose from the fact that there were blessings offered for obedience and curses

---

64   The hymn 'Make me a captive' by George Matheson (1842-1906).

65   Makkot.23B, the Babylonian Talmud. Trans.Rabbi Dr. I. Epstein. Brooklyn: Soncino Press, 1938.

66   Isaac Broide and Kaufmann Kohler, "The 613 Commandments" in the Jewish Encyclopedia.com.

threatened for disobedience, as vocalized by Moses himself. *"Behold, I set before you today a blessing and a curse: the blessing, if you obey the commandments of the Lord your God which I command you today; and the curse, if you do not obey the commandments of the Lord your God"* (Deut 11:26-28).

This momentous event, the giving of the Law, seems to have unfolded in the following order.

1. In the third month after their exodus from Egypt they arrived at Mount Sinai. Moses had known from the time of his call that Israel would meet God there.[67] On arrival, they encamped at the foot of the mountain. The Lord descended from heaven and made Himself available at the peak of the mountain. Several meteorological signs attended his presence. Then He called Moses into His presence and made an offer of a special relationship, a relationship in which Israel would be (a)   His 'special treasure',[68] *'segulah'* in Hebrew, the private property of a king, as distinct from that used for public purposes, as with David in 1 Chron. 29:3 (emphasis added) *"Moreover, because I have set my affection on the house of my God, I have given to the house of my God, over and above all that I have prepared for the holy house, **my own special treasure** of gold and silver."* Israel was to be God's 'special treasure'. This particular and peculiar relationship is referred to again in Deuteronomy; *"For you are a holy people to the Lord your God; the Lord your God has chosen you to be a people for Himself, a special treasure above all the peoples on the face of the earth"* (Deut. 7:6); and *"you are a holy people to the Lord your God, and the Lord has chosen you to be a people for Himself, a special treasure above all the peoples who are on the face of the earth"* (Deut. 14:2); and *"the Lord has proclaimed you to be His special people, just as He promised you, that you should keep all His commandments"* (Deut. 26:18). It is of great importance to the

---

67   Ex. 3:12
68   Ex. 19:5

nation, preceding as it does, the giving of the Law. (b) *"And you shall be to Me a kingdom of priests"* (Ex. 19:6). This implied more than a priestly caste, and indeed later Jewish tradition understood it as such, converting it from a promise to a responsibility (noblesse oblige), and requiring the whole population to live by the same code of holiness that the priests lived by. This formed part of the background to the conflict between the Messiah and the Pharisees. (c) *"and a holy nation"* (Ex 19:6). A nation that could discern between holy and unholy, between clean and unclean.[69]

2. Moses descended the mountain and made the offer, on behalf of the LORD, to the elders and people of Israel, who accepted it without hesitation.[70] Moses then returned to the presence of the LORD and relayed the response of the nation.[71]

3. Now that the people had agreed to enter into the special relationship, preparations had to be made that would formalize and itemize the agreement, so the LORD issued instructions that the people should prepare themselves by bathing, laundering and preparing their hearts to hear His Word. In addition, as God commanded, boundaries were set around the mountain. He had to charge the people to keep their place and ensure the sanctity of those that had been fulfilling a priestly office.[72]

4. After these preparations, on the morning of the third day (from the issuing of this divine command), the LORD came down upon the top of Mount Sinai, manifesting His glory in fire, in the midst of thunders and lightnings. The mountain burned with fire and trembled like a leaf. These natural phenomena were accom-

---

69   Lev. 10:10
70   Ex. 19:8
71   Ex. 19:8
72   Ex. 19:20

panied by a loud trumpet blast, which *"sounded long and became louder and louder"* (Ex. 19:19). This *'Tekiah Gedolah'* as it would be called at the Feast of Trumpets, had two main purposes. The first purpose was to announce the arrival of the LORD, and the second, to summon the nation to assemble before Him and listen to His words.

5. At this time the LORD summoned Moses into His presence to further impress on him the solemnity of the occasion, and the need to emphasize to the people that they were to keep their station, on risk of death.

6. After Moses had returned to the foot of the mountain, God spoke to the nation the 'ten words' of the Decalogue.[73] Forty years later, the aged prophet, recalling the event, said, *"The LORD talked with you face to face on the mountain from the midst of the fire"* (Deut. 5:4). The whole of the Mosaic covenant would rest on these ten commands – they would be its foundation.

7. Experiencing the LORD so close was overpowering for the nation. The command to draw near was still in effect. *"When the trumpet sounds long, they shall come near the mountain"* (Ex 19:13). They were expecting another long trumpet blast to call them into the near presence of God. The phenomena attending His presence overawed the people. They cried, *"You speak with us, and we will hear; but let not God speak with us, lest we die"* (Ex. 20:19). In such a manner was Moses finally established as the mediator between God and Israel.

8. The establishing of Moses as Israel's mediator needed to be repeated for Aaron who was soon to be inducted as the High Priest of the nation. So Moses again ascended the mountain—this time with Aaron.[74] While Aaron stood afar off, Moses drew near to the LORD, and received a communication. *"Thus you shall*

---

73   Ex. 20:1-17
74   Ex. 19:24

*say to the children of Israel: 'You have seen that I have talked
with you from heaven. You shall not make anything to be
with Me—gods of silver or gods of gold you shall not make
for yourselves. An altar of earth you shall make for Me, and
you shall sacrifice on it your burnt offerings and your peace
offerings, your sheep and your oxen. In every place where
I record My name I will come to you, and I will bless you.
And if you make Me an altar of stone, you shall not build it
of hewn stone; for if you use your tool on it, you have pro-
faned it. Nor shall you go up by steps to My altar, that your
nakedness may not be exposed on it'"* (Ex. 20:22-26).

9. This new message was to be transmitted to the nation.
    It included a re-emphasizing of that element of the
    Decalogue that forbade idolatry as well as images that
    were meant to represent the LORD. Israel was not only
    banned from making, owning or worshipping images
    of other gods but also banned from making, owning or
    worshipping images intended to be some form of rep-
    resentation of the God of Israel. As the *Sh'ma* begins,
    "Hear, O Israel: The LORD our God, the LORD is one!" (Deut.
    6:4). This is understood to mean that the LORD is the
    One absolute God, therefore worshipping other gods
    is not only forbidden but also foolish. Furthermore,
    *"God is Spirit, and those who worship Him must worship
    in spirit and truth"* (John 4:24). Again, seeking to repre-
    sent in some physical and material form the One who
    is Spirit, is not only forbidden, but also foolish.

10. Along with these fresh instructions was the command
    to bring the elders, together with Aaron, Nadab and
    Abihu, up the mountain. When Moses returned to
    relay this fresh intelligence to the nation, they again
    responded, *"All the words which the LORD has said we
    will do"* (Ex. 24:3). This was enough for Moses to pro-
    ceed to consolidate the agreement between the LORD
    and the nation. This Moses did the following morning.

11. With the latest guidance, regarding the building of an altar to the LORD, fresh in his mind, Moses rose early the next morning and set about the work formalizing the covenant that was to be cut between the nation and the LORD. He built an altar together with twelve pillars to represent the twelve tribes of Israel. In addition, he composed a book in which he wrote both the promises and the precepts that had initially been communicated to him.

12. Then in a formal ceremony in which many young men of Israel acted as priests, burnt offerings and peace offerings were presented to God. Half the blood from the animal sacrifices was used to consecrate the altar.

13. After reading to the assembled people the detailed covenant which had been offered and verbally accepted, he waited until they again declared, *"All that the LORD has said we will do, and be obedient"* (Ex. 24:7). At this point, Moses took the remaining blood, and swinging it around, sprinkled it on the people, and said, *"This is the blood of the covenant which the LORD has made with you according to all these words"* (Ex. 24:8).

14. Now came the time to fulfill the command to bring Aaron, Nadab, Abihu and the elders up the mountain to meet with God. Having been consecrated by the blood of the covenant, the elders and those that would initialize the priesthood then drew near. The covenant between the LORD and those representing Israel was celebrated with a sacramental meal, during which there was a theophany. The mechanics of the vision are not divulged. The plain statement of Scripture is, *"they saw the God of Israel"* (Ex. 24:10). A little more is added, *"And there was under His feet as it were a paved work of sapphire stone, and it was like the very heavens in its clarity"* (Ex. 24:10). At the end of the covenantal meal, the representatives of Israel, along with Moses left the mountain.

15. But all was not yet complete. There was much more to communicate regarding this covenant, especially that which related to the priesthood, the offerings and the sanctuary. It would require the presence of Moses for a much longer time. *"Then the LORD said to Moses, 'Come up to Me on the mountain and be there; and I will give you tablets of stone, and the law and commandments which I have written, that you may teach them'"* (Ex. 24:12). It seems Moses had an idea that this stay on the mountain would be an extended period because he appointed Aaron and Hur as judges in his absence, and took Joshua with him to serve him.[75]

16. Joshua and Moses ascended the mountain whose summit was now covered by a cloud in which the glory of God resided. This glory tarried in the cloud for seven days and appeared to the Israelites in the camp below like devouring fire (cf. 19:16). On the seventh day; the LORD called Moses into the cloud. Whether Joshua followed him we are not told, but it is evident from Ex. 32:17 that he was with him on the mountain, though, judging from v. 2 and Ex. 33:11, he did not go into the immediate presence of God.

17. Moses was on the mountain for forty days and forty nights, during which time he neither ate nor drank.[76] There are some powerful associations that spring to mind in connection with the forty days and forty nights, not least of all because it was a period that Moses had to repeat.[77] Elijah took forty days to journey to this very mountain on the strength of one meal only.[78] Goliath's challenge to Israel was over a period

---

75   Ex. 24:13-14
76   Deut. 9:9
77   Ex. 34:28; Deut. 9:18
78   1 Kings 19:8

of forty days,[79] as was the challenge of Satan during the fast of Jesus in the wilderness.[80]

18. During this extended period on the mountain, Moses received instructions regarding the building of the Tabernacle, the making of its furniture for which the LORD promised the provision of skilled workers and the consecration of a Priesthood and instructions regarding daily offerings. Though the Tabernacle would be necessary for the spiritual welfare of the whole nation, it was not designed for communal use. It is after some instructions regarding the daily offerings that the encounter is first summed up in Ex. 29:43-46: "... *there I will meet with the children of Israel, and the tabernacle shall be sanctified by My glory. So I will consecrate the tabernacle of meeting and the altar. I will also consecrate both Aaron and his sons to minister to Me as priests. I will dwell among the children of Israel and will be their God. And they shall know that I am the LORD their God, who brought them up out of the land of Egypt, that I may dwell among them. I am the LORD their God"* (Ex 29:43-46). The end of the encounter is given in Ex. 31:18. *"And He gave unto Moses, when he had made an end of communing with him upon mount Sinai, two tables of testimony, tables of stone, written with the finger of God."*

A Summary of the Law

The law itself was in three sections—commandments, judgments and ordinances. It provided a code of conduct and rule of law that brought order and structure to allow them to function, not as twelve separate tribes, but as one nation, as well as providing the sacerdotal organization in which their relationship with the LORD might flourish. Here are some examples:

---

79   1 Sam. 17:16
80   Matt. 4:2; Luke 4:2

Commandments (Ex. 20.2-17)

The Decalogue is the foundation of the Law.

"I am the LORD *your God, who brought you out of the land of Egypt, out of the house of bondage. "You shall have no other gods before Me.*

"You shall not make for yourself a carved image—any likeness of anything that is in heaven above, or that is in the earth beneath, or that is in the water under the earth; you shall not bow down to them nor serve them. For I, the LORD *your God, am a jealous God, visiting the iniquity of the fathers upon the children to the third and fourth generations of those who hate Me, but showing mercy to thousands, to those who love Me and keep My commandments.*

"You shall not take the name of the LORD *your God in vain, for the* LORD *will not hold him guiltless who takes His name in vain.*

"Remember the Sabbath day, to keep it holy. Six days you shall labour and do all your work, but the seventh day is the Sabbath of the LORD *your God. In it you shall do no work: you, nor your son, nor your daughter, nor your male servant, nor your female servant, nor your cattle, nor your stranger who is within your gates. For in six days the* LORD *made the heavens and the earth, the sea, and all that is in them, and rested the seventh day. Therefore the* LORD *blessed the Sabbath day and hallowed it.*

"Honour your father and your mother, that your days may be long upon the land which the LORD *your God is giving you.*

"You shall not murder.

"You shall not commit adultery.

"You shall not steal.

"You shall not bear false witness against your neighbour.

"You shall not covet your neighbour's house; you shall not covet your neighbor's wife, nor his male servant, nor his female servant, nor his ox, nor his donkey, nor anything that is your neighbour's."

This section is famously summarized by the Messiah. When asked, *"Teacher, which is the great commandment in the law?"* Jesus answered, *"'You shall love the* LORD *your God with all your heart, with all your soul, and with all your mind.' This is the first and great commandment. And the second is like it: 'You shall love your neighbor as yourself.' On these two commandments hang all the Law ...*" (Matt. 22:36-40).

Judgments

The second category, coming under the general description 'judgments', deal with social requirements[81] (Ex. 21:1-23). It begins, "*Now these are the judgments which you shall set before them.*" Examples include, "*If you buy a Hebrew servant, he shall serve six years; and in the seventh he shall go out free and pay nothing. If he comes in by himself, he shall go out by himself; if he comes in married, then his wife shall go out with him. If his master has given him a wife, and she has borne him sons or daughters, the wife and her children shall be her master's, and he shall go out by himself*" (Ex. 21:2-4). There are regulations concerning the punishment to be inflicted for the taking of a life deliberately, and the compensation to be paid for the taking of a life accidentally. They not only deal with the loss and impairing of human life, but also animal life. This is given importance since the nation would continue to be an agricultural society. Also promulgated are detailed laws dealing with stealing, cheating and telling untruths, as also encouragements to deal kindly with strangers and the poor. These laws are designed to produce a nation that would reflect the righteousness and mercy of the LORD.

Ordinances

The third category is 'ordinances'. These regulate the worship, that is, the activities of the priesthood and the ordering of the calendar to include annual festivals;[82] examples include the construction of the Tabernacle and its furniture. It was designed to have three main areas, each with a different degree of holiness, and each with a specific purpose. In the outer court there would be a laver to hold water for the priests' ablutions and a metal altar on which sacrifices could be offered. Inside the tent shrine were two rooms, the first was the holy place containing

---

81   Ex. 21:1-23
82   Ex. 25:1 to 31:18

a golden altar, a golden seven branch Menorah[83] which was oil fired, and a golden table designed to hold the bread of the Presence. The 'ordinances' section includes regulations to do with the ordering of its services, the consecration of a priesthood and the description of permitted offerings. Offerings were designed either for expiation and propitiation, that is, sin offerings, or as 'sweet savour' offerings for acceptance as worship. The timing and activities of the religious festivals were also designated ordinances and had to be observed in a set way since they had the authority of the Law behind them. The main festivals were the feast of Passover (*Hag HaPesach*); the feast of Unleavened Bread (*Hag HaMatzot*h); the feast of Firstfruits (*Hag HaBikkurim*); the feast of Weeks (*Hag HaShavu'ot*); the feast of Trumpets (*Hag HaTruah*); the Day of Atonement (*Yom Kippur*); the feast of Tabernacles (*Hag HaSukkoth*); and the Sabbath (*Shabbat*).[84]

---

83   lampstand

84   For a larger treatment of the Feasts of the Lord see The Messiah and the Feasts of Israel Gospel Folio Press, Port Colborne, 2006, by the same author.

Chapter 6
The Mosaic Covenant – Its Purpose and Effect

The Israelites, when they were redeemed from Egypt, were a disorganized group of tribes, with poor leadership and almost no government. There was very little commitment to their leaders. Decisions could be queried – sometimes even rejected. There was little coordinated action amongst them. But crisis had brought them together. The Egyptians had increased their suffering as they themselves suffered under the barrage of plagues inflicted from heaven. Adversity had bound Israel closer together as a unit. When they left their homes, with their backs towards Egypt and their faces towards Canaan, there would be new challenges before them. The new spirit of unity required consolidating and the nation needed structure and government. Moreover, if they were to meet enemies, they would need an army with order and discipline.

God, of course, was always working to a plan. Israel would be constituted as a kingdom, which was intended to be a pattern of the kingdom which is yet to grace the earth, the millennial kingdom under Israel's Messiah, the Son of God. The leadership of the kingdom of Israel would reside in three anointed offices. Since the government of the nation would be a theocracy, the king, chosen by the LORD, would be answerable to Him. In this situation, the king would require support in two areas. Obviously, he would need to know the mind of God; this would be the domain of the prophet. He would come with messages from the throne, prefacing his utterances with the phrase, *"Thus says the LORD."*[85] This would also allow the LORD to make progress with His plan to mould the nation into a receptacle that would

---

85   There are 416 reference in 414 verses to this phrase in the *T'nach* (Old Testament).

suit the incarnation. The first great prophet for the nation was, of course, Moses. He brought the mind of God to Israel at the time of the birth of the nation. And, even as the Tabernacle was a shadow of good things to come, so also Moses was to be a foreshadowing of the Messiah who would come.[86] The second line of support for the king would come from the priesthood – in particular, the High Priest - who would intercede for the king and the people. Aaron and the Aaronic priesthood would also foreshadow the priestly ministry of the Messiah, and because of that, would educate the nation to understand and embrace the doctrines of substitution and forgiveness which were necessary if a meaningful relationship between them and their God could prosper. The main authority would rest with the king, but he would be supported by the prophet and priest.

With the first part of the redemption of the nation from Egypt behind them, God began the process of establishing the three lines of leadership. The intimacy of Moses with God sanctified him in the eyes of the people. His position as prophet was beyond question. The selection of Aaron by God, and his interview on the mountain, established him as High Priest. Initially, God Himself assumed the third role, that of sovereign LORD.

Clearly, if these people, descendents of Abraham, were to fulfill the high ambition that the LORD had for them, and also to be a witness to the surrounding nations, then a moral, ethical and social code by which to live was a necessity. Their leaders would need instruction on how to provide an environment that would be safe and equitable for its nationals. This nation, now constituted 'the people of God', is to be the cradle into which the Son of God will be born, so its administration will need to provide the conditions in which He could be raised in accordance with holy principles to live a holy life. Moses and Aaron, together with the elders of Israel, could have gone into conclave and produced some kind of constitution that would have been the basis for their legal and sacerdotal regimes, but that did not happen. This people, now separated to the God of Abraham, were privileged to have the Law disclosed directly from Him,

---

86   Deut. 18:15

and since He personally promulgated the code, it owned an authority that no other code could possess. He issued it in its entirety, amid great spectacles of majesty and glory. There was no human involvement other than using a mediator to receive and pass on what was His will. Moses, at no time, entered the presence of the LORD with a list of suggestions or requests. The Mosaic Law was entirely God's idea, and therefore had the backing of Omniscience.

The Law as a Wall of Separation

Sometimes it is said, "It is not so much that Israel keeps the Sabbath but the Sabbath keeps Israel." What this suggests is that the Law of Moses was an instrument that was used to separate the Jewish race from all other nations. There is much in Scripture to support this. The benefits that are available to the people of God were only accessible by those who embraced the Law of Moses. The Temple itself was a physical example of the separation. While Gentiles were welcomed on the Temple Mount and indeed into the Temple itself, they could only enter the court of Gentiles, and as observers at that. This court, the most outer of all the courts, was separated from all other areas of the Temple by a four foot six inch wall. In the wall there were thirteen openings through which Jews were admitted but Gentiles were barred. The openings were guarded by Levites and inscriptions in Latin and Greek were posted at each of the openings. In 1871 a limestone notice was discovered in Jerusalem which read, 'No stranger is to enter within the balustrade around the Temple and its enclosure. Whoever is caught will be responsible for his own death, which will ensue'.[87] Paul alluded to this wall in his letter to the Ephesians, when he said, *"For He Himself is our peace, who has made both one, and has broken down the middle wall of separation"* (Eph 2:14).

Paul taught that the Mosaic Law was intended to maintain the separation of the Jewish people to the God of Abraham. The blessings of the Abrahamic Covenant were not available

---

87   Alec Garrard, <u>The Splendour of the Temple,</u> (Moat Farm Publications, 1997) p.46.

to Gentiles unless they embraced fully all that it meant to be a Jew, including, for the men, being circumcised. He describes the condition of those that were not Jewish; *"At that time you were ... aliens from the commonwealth of Israel and strangers from the covenants of promise, having no hope and without God in the world"* (Eph. 2:12-13).

A Diagram showing Jews and Gentiles
Separated by the Mosaic Covenant

JEWS	Law of Moses	GENTILES
Abrahamic Covenant Promised Seed/Land/Blessings	(a wall of partion)	Strangers to the Covenants of promise

The Law was limited in its ability to deal with sin

The Day of Atonement (*Yom Kippur*) was, and still is, the most important day in the religious calendar of Israel. It falls on the 10th *Tishri*. The instructions for the Day are in Leviticus 23:26-32, with some repetition in Numbers 29:7-11 where the ritual offerings are listed. Leviticus 16:29-34 also refers to this Day where the emphasis there is on the priest who performs the ceremony in the Tabernacle. This day is at the heart of the Mosaic Covenant. Among the Jewish people it has long been considered that the first Yom Kippur took place after Moses had received the second set of stone tablets on which were the Ten Commandments. After the sin of the golden calf,[88] the nation fasted and waited in repentance while Moses ascended the mountain to intercede for them. He returned on the 10th *Tishri* to announce that God had forgiven the nation, in honour of which the 10th *Tishri* would remain a day of atonement for all generations. The Day of Atonement was always significant in the national calendar, but after the Babylonian exile, it took on much greater importance in the culture of Israel. Since the exile

---

88   Ex. 32:1 ff

was considered a judgement of God because the nation had failed to keep the Mosaic Law, then fulfilling the Law, especially as it applied to this key Temple service in which atonement was made for the sins of the people, became vital. Because the daily sacrifices were unable to deal with all sins, particularly secret sins, the sacrifices on the Day of Atonement became the major offerings of the religious year. The basic idea was a 'covering' for sin, the purpose of which was to accomplish reconciliation between God and man.

The Hebrew word whereby the doctrine of the atonement is usually set out in the Old Testament is *'kaphar'*, the original meaning of which was 'to cover' or 'to shelter'. Strong's Hebrew dictionary has 'to cover' as the initial meaning in all forms of the word. "**1 to cover**, purge, make an atonement, make reconciliation, cover over with pitch. 1A (Qal) **to coat or cover with pitch**. 1B (Piel). *1B1* **to cover over**, pacify, propitiate. *1B2* **to cover over**, atone for sin, make atonement for. *1B3* **to cover over**, atone for sin and persons by legal rites. 1c (Pual). *1c1* **to be covered over**. *1c2* to make atonement for. 1D (Hithpael) **to be covered**" (Strongs No. 3722). The name of the mercyseat, *'kapporeth'* is derived from *'kaphar,'* and is itself a covering, a lid to the ark of the covenant, in which was kept the two tablets of stone on which were engraved the Decalogue, the foundation of the Law of God.

What is suggested here is the truth that the sacrificial system as utilized by the Levitical priesthood could not cleanse sin, only cover it. This is a distinct weakness in the economy that prevailed during the dispensation of Law. The writer of the Hebrew letter remarks on this weakness. *"For it is not possible that the blood of bulls and goats could take away sins"* (Heb. 10:4).

Summary

The Mosaic Law was initially designed:

a. to bring order and discipline to the nation.

b. to provide rules for righteous living and righteous behavior.

c. to provide a way of repairing the relationship with God (for both individuals and the nation) when that relationship had fractured because of sin.

d. to keep the nation free from the contamination of other idolatrous nations, whose idea of righteousness did not rise to the heights demanded by the God of the Hebrews.

e. to educate and train the nation in such a way that it would be ready and prepared, in the fullness of time, to receive its Messiah, who would also be the Saviour of the world.

What the Law was not designed to do was to provide a permanent rule for righteous living, nor a permanent answer to the problem of sin.

Chapter 7
The Land Covenant

In the Abrahamic Covenant there is mention of a homeland for the posterity of Abraham.[89] At the time when Abraham had confidence that his children, and his children's children, would multiply into a large nation (he had believed God and it had been accounted to him for righteousness)[90] he re-visited the issue of where they would live. Several times he had been promised the land bordering the Mediterranean as a homeland for them,[91] but that seemed very improbable – it was already occupied, and the inhabitants were very well established. Abraham appealed to God for some assurance, and the LORD gave him that assurance under the ceremony of 'cutting a covenant', at the end of which He said, *"To your descendants I **have given this land**, from the river of Egypt to the great river, the River Euphrates— the Kenites, the Kenezzites, the Kadmonites, the Hittites, the Perizzites, the Rephaim, the Amorites, the Canaanites, the Girgashites, and the Jebusites"* (Gen. 15:18-21, emphasis added). Thus the promise of the land is a main feature of the covenant of God with Abraham. This is not the Land Covenant; this is the land aspect of the Abrahamic Covenant.

Title to the land of Canaan was renewed with Isaac. *"**Dwell in this land**, and I will be with you and bless you; for **to you and your descendants I give all these lands**, and I will perform the oath which I swore to Abraham your father"* (Gen.26:3, emphasis added) Hand in hand with the title of the land was the promise of the blessing of the LORD, which makes rich and adds no

---

89   Gen. 15:7
90   Gen. 15:5-6
91   Gen. 12:7; 13:15; 13:17; 15:7

sorrow with it.[92] *"Then Isaac sowed in that land, and reaped in the same year a hundredfold; and the LORD blessed him"* (Gen. 26:12).

Isaac, in turn, conferred both blessing and title on Jacob, who would be renamed Israel. *"Then Isaac called Jacob and blessed him ... and said to him ... May God Almighty bless you, And make you fruitful and multiply you, That you may be an assembly of peoples; And give you the **blessing of Abraham**, To you and your descendants with you, **That you may inherit the land** In which you are a stranger, Which God gave to Abraham."* (Gen. 28:1-5, emphasis added).

And God confirmed it to Jacob at Bethel, saying, *"I am the LORD God of Abraham your father and the God of Isaac; **the land on which you lie I will give to you and your descendants**"* (Gen. 28:13, emphasis added). Jacob returned to Bethel where God changed his name to Israel and renewed entitlement to the land.[93] It is to this experience that he returned when speaking to Joseph when Joseph was a ruler in Egypt; *"Then Jacob said to Joseph: 'God Almighty appeared to me at Luz in the land of Canaan and blessed me, and said to me, 'Behold, I will make you fruitful and multiply you, and I will make of you a multitude of people, and **give this land to your descendants after you as an everlasting possession**'"* (Gen. 48:3-4, emphasis added). Joseph, clearly aware of the covenant and confident that it would mature in due time, gave instruction for his remains to be taken and buried in the land of promise when God led the nation of Israel out of Egypt.[94]

The detail of the Abrahamic Covenant dictated that the grant of the land should not mature until more than four centuries after Israel had resided in Egypt. Accordingly, it is during the time of Moses that the promise of the land of Canaan to Israel comes to the fore. Moses, chosen by God to be deliverer, mediator and leader, had a message for Israel. It was in two parts. The first related to the deliverance – God would bring them out. The second would relate to their inheritance – God would take them in to Canaan. The intelligence given at 'the bush' included this double purpose of the LORD. *"I have come*

---

92   Prov. 10:22
93   Gen 35:12
94   Gen. 50:24-25

down **to deliver them out** *of the hand of the Egyptians, and* **to bring them up** *from that land* **to a good and large land, to a land flowing with milk and honey,** *to the place of the Canaanites and the Hittites and the Amorites and the Perizzites and the Hivites and the Jebusites"* (Ex. 3:8). The provision of God was to be of the highest quality. The land is described as 'good', which to a nation whose economy was to be agricultural, meant 'fertile'; it is 'broad' in contrast to the confinement of their Egyptian prison; and flowing with 'milk and honey', which are the choicest products of a land with abundant grass and flowers. This last epithet, 'flowing with milk and honey', is the descriptive phrase that is most frequently employed to summarize the fruitfulness of what was to be the new homeland of the Jewish nation.[95]

The generation that was redeemed from Egypt did not receive this second part of the message in faith, and were excluded from Canaan (all except Caleb and Joshua). But even unbelief and disobedience cannot annul an unconditional covenant, (the Abrahamic Covenant held this status), and they did ultimately enter the land. But Moses, God's prophet and spokesman, indicated that their occupation of the land would be conditional. This became evident when the land element of the Abrahamic Covenant was then redrafted as a covenant in its own right. Although mediated by Moses, it was separate from the Mosaic Covenant; *"These are the words of the covenant which the* LORD *commanded Moses to make with the children of Israel in the land of Moab,* **besides the covenant which He made with them in Horeb"** (Deut. 29:1, emphasis added). And the terms were spelt out in great detail.[96]

In that part of his address recorded in chapters 28 through 30 of Deuteronomy, Moses had been at pains to warn the nation that they would lose occupation of the land if they disobeyed the Mosaic covenant. In fact, he prophesied that some time in the future they would turn away from the LORD, and be exiled

---

95   Ex. 3:8,17; 13:5; 33:3; Lev. 20:24; Numb. 13:27; 14:8; 16. 13-14; Deut. 6:3; 11:9; 26:9,15; 27:3; 31:20; Josh. 5:6; Jer. 11:5; 32:22; Ezek.20.6,15

96   Deut. 29:1 ff.

from the land, but it would not invalidate either the Abrahamic Covenant or the Land Covenant, for God would, on their repentance, regather them and return them to the land, even if they had been scattered to the four corners of the earth.

So the Abrahamic covenant declared that title to the land was unconditional.

The Land Covenant declared that occupation of the land was conditioned on the obedience of the Jewish nation.

It appears from chapter 30 of Deuteronomy that the Land Covenant will only come into full fruition during the Messianic age, that period when Israel would have come to realize and accept that Jesus of Nazareth is their Messiah and LORD.

Warfare and Welfare

The land was to be ordered as a kingdom, where each inhabitant had a place, with security and benefits, and where they would be able to fulfill responsibilities and perform duties. It is the book of Joshua that describes the entering, conquest and settling of the 'promised land'. The book can be divided into two halves. Chapters 1 to 12 deal with the conquest of the land, and describe Israel's *warfare*. Then chapters 13 to 24 deal with the division of the land, which is *welfare*. The first half mainly concerns the **strategy of warfare.** It describes the three main campaigns of the army. The second half concerns the **structure of welfare**, which was the division of the inheritance and the placing of the cities of refuge.

The Strategy of Warfare

In the strategy of warfare, victory depended **on purity**. Disobedience in warfare is a capital offence. In God's army it is called 'sin' and was committed by Achan.[97] The key issue here is the breaking of the very covenant into which they had so recently entered wholeheartedly. They had said, *"All that the LORD has spoken we will do."* (Ex. 19:8; 24:7) But so soon on

---

97   Joshua chapter 7

entering the land under a covenant relationship with the LORD, the covenant is under threat. Achan's sin was first covetousness, (*"you shall not covet"* is the 10th commandment of the Decalogue); theft; (*"You shall not steal"* is the eighth commandment); and his theft was of the worse kind because it was taking for personal use, something dedicated to the LORD. Added to that was concealment and lying, which was against the essence of the ninth commandment, *"you shall not bear false witness"*. The army was weakened and defeated as a direct result. The situation was only recovered when the 'treason' was discovered and punished.

In God's army victory depends **on unity** as well as purity. An indirect result of Achan's sin was that the army was divided for this time only. As a consequence of the trespass committed at Jericho, Joshua failed to realize that the presence of the LORD was not with them as before. He did not seek guidance, and relied on his army to accomplish victory. Sending only enough men as were needed for victory, or so he thought, his army was routed. It was only after they had purged the sin of Achan was the army able to resume their campaign. Never again, in the invasion of Canaan, did Joshua divide his army.

Furthermore, victory also depends **on recovery**. After each campaign the army returned to Gilgal, there to rest, recover and restore their weapons to battle condition. They did not go from campaign to campaign. Gilgal, of course, was where the ark was kept.

The application of these truths is clear. For those engaged in spiritual warfare the importance of individual obedience, corporate unity and universal communion cannot be over-emphasized.

But even though their three pronged campaign was successful, the conquest was still only partial. This was not by chance but a part of God's strategy in the education of the nation. When the Land Covenant was granted, Israel was still a pilgrim nation in the wilderness. They were instructed to possess the land by conquest, but it would only be achieved if they had faith in the LORD. The conquest would be progressive and not immediate. In other words, on their part it would not be one act of faith but a continuing life of faith that would obtain Canaan as their homeland; *"I will not drive them out from before you in one year, lest the land become desolate and the beasts of the field become too numerous for you. Little by little I will drive them out from before you, until you have increased, and you inherit the land. And I will set your bounds from the Red Sea to the sea, Philistia, and from the desert to the River. For I will deliver the inhabitants of the land into your hand, and you shall drive them out before you* (Ex. 23:29-31).

And since they had been given title to the land in the grace and gift of the LORD, then their conduct and actions needed to reflect His character - they were to act with justice and with mercy; *"And if a stranger dwells with you in your land, you shall not mistreat him. The stranger who dwells among you shall be to you as one born among you, and you shall love him as yourself; for you were strangers in the land of Egypt:* **I am the LORD your God**. *You shall do no injustice in judgment, in measurement of length, weight, or volume. You shall have honest scales, honest weights, an honest ephah, and an honest hin:* **I am the LORD your God**, *who brought you out of the land of Egypt"* (Lev. 19:33-36, emphasis added).

Moreover, it was required that they not repeat the folly of the Canaanites. The culture of the Canaanites, the Hittites, the Amorites, the Perizzites, the Hivites and the Jebusites had been condemned by the LORD which was the reason for their expulsion from Canaan. *"Do not defile yourselves with any of these things; for by all these the nations are defiled, which I am casting out before you. For the land is defiled; therefore I visit the punishment of its iniquity upon it, and the land vomits out its inhabitants. You shall therefore keep My statutes and My judgments, and shall not commit any of these abominations, either any of your own nation or any stranger who dwells among you (for all these abominations the men of the land have done, who were before you, and thus the land is defiled)"* (Lev. 18:24-27). Indeed, the period of time that Israel spent in Egypt was partly dictated by the need to wait until the Canaanites were ripe for judgement, as indicated at the 'cutting' of the Abrahamic Covenant, the ceremony which provided entitlement of Canaan as a homeland for Israel.[98] The promised terri-

---

98   Gen. 15:16 (Amorites is used as a general term for the

tory remained a 'pleasant land';[99] an 'exceeding good land';[100] a land flowing with 'milk and honey',[101] even though the inhabitants were evacuated because of their culture.

But if possession of the land was conditional for Israel, so was blessing. The land, in which the 'seed' of Abraham was to be transplanted, would only remain fruitful and give of its strength if the occupants remained faithful to the LORD: *"If you walk in My statutes and keep My commandments, and perform them, then I will give you rain in its season, the land shall yield its produce, and the trees of the field shall yield their fruit"* (Lev. 26:3-4). If they apostatized, *"you shall sow your seed in vain"* and *"your enemies shall eat it"* (Lev. 26:16). Furthermore, *"your strength shall be spent in vain; for your land shall not yield its produce, nor shall the trees of the land yield their fruit"* (Lev. 26:20).

The structure of Welfare

Dividing the inheritance. Caleb and Joshua had some advantage in securing a sweet portion of the land because they had been there before. However, some of the nation sought their portion the other side of Jordan, outside the Promised Land. They were the first to receive their allocation, but they were also the first to lose it. And the Levites, the tribe that were in the service of the LORD did not get a portion of the land as such, on the principle that the LORD was their portion, but they were allocated cities of refuge which were placed strategically throughout the territory.

Israel was to be a society ordered by God and every aspect of their possession and husbandry of the land was governed by God's law. Examples include:

- Land division, landmarks, ownership, mortgage and redemption of mortgages.

Canaanite nations)
99   Ps. 106:24
100   Num. 14:7
101   Ex. 3:8,17; 13:5; 33:3; Lev. 20:24; Num. 13:27; 14:8; 16:13,14; Deut. 6:3; 11:9; 26:9,15; 27:3; 31:20

- A Sabbath rest for the land every seven years.
- The method of harvesting and gleaning.
- Their harvest festivals as a constant reminder.
- Their tithes and offerings.
- Control of nature and wild animals.

This aspect of righteous behavior was emphasized by Moses when he addressed the nation before he died. What he explained was that it was not their righteousness that would obtain the land initially. It would be the grace of God. He said, *"Do not think in your heart, after the LORD your God has cast them out before you, saying, 'Because of my righteousness the LORD has brought me in to possess this land'; but it is because of the wickedness of these nations that the LORD is driving them out from before you. It is not because of your righteousness or the uprightness of your heart that you go in to possess their land, but because of the wickedness of these nations that the LORD your God drives them out from before you, and that He may fulfill the word which the LORD swore to your fathers, to Abraham, Isaac, and Jacob. Therefore understand that the LORD your God is not giving you this good land to possess because of your righteousness, for you are a stiff-necked people"* (Deut. 9:4-6). But it would be their obedience that would keep them in it. Moreover, obedience would bring them great benefit.[102] The benefit was encompassed in the word 'blessing' and would touch all aspects of life. They would be blessed in the city and in the country, that is, the two spheres in which their life would be lived. There would be fruitfulness in offspring, in their own families and in the animals that they owned. The produce of the ground would be blessed, as would their storehouses and domestic instruments, indeed the nation would be blessed in all its undertakings, both when under threat or at peace. The LORD would give them rain in its season, and the blessing of the LORD would make them rich so that they would be lenders and not borrowers. All these benefits when brought together would make Israel a leader among the nations.

---

102   Deut. 28:1-14

The Covenant relationship between Israel and her God was re-enforced after Israel had begun occupation of their new homeland. As Moses addressed the nation before he died, so also Joshua. He called the leaders of the tribes to Shechem, the place that was the site of important patriarchal experiences. It was here that Abraham received the first promise of the land, whereupon Abram (as his name was then) built an altar[103] and thereby sanctified the ground under the oak (or terebinth). It was here that Jacob purified his house on his return to the land. He buried the foreign idols that had been brought with them under the tree.[104] So it would be at this very same site that the Covenant relationship would be strengthened. Joshua, speaking for the LORD, recited the history of their people beginning with the call of Abraham and ending with the giving of the land and, on the basis of this, challenged the people to choose who they would serve. Joshua, great leader as he was, led the way by declaring he had already chosen. He would serve the LORD. When the people also declared their allegiance, *"we also will serve the LORD, for He is our God"* (Josh. 24:18), Joshua reminded them of the gravity of their decision and made a covenant for them which was written and preserved with the covenants previously declared.[105]

That Israel is a covenant society cannot be doubted. Beginning with Abraham, renewed with Jacob, re-established through Moses and now again with Joshua, every confidence Israel exhibits in the future must be seen as the result of their covenant relationship with the LORD.

---

103   Gen. 12:6-7
104   Gen. 35:4
105   Josh. 24:25-26

Chapter 8
The Land Covenant -
Its Purpose and Effect

Canaan was to be a home for Israel, a home that would be a place of safety and peace where they could live in comfort—a place where there would be food and drink to sustain them, and a place to provide protection from outside influences. Canaan was all this to them— a fertile and well watered country that provided a balanced diet for its occupants. The peace and safety was provided by the Lord.

But since the Land Covenant, which had expanded the land aspect of the Abrahamic Covenant, had made the occupation of Canaan conditional on obedience and faith, it was also an incentive to godly living. And as an incentive it was of five star quality - walk with God or lose your homeland – it could not be clearer. Moses, God's spokesman, inspired in his oratory, reminded the nation that exile awaited any generation that turned from the Lord. Having used the carrot, that is, declaring that obedience brought blessing, he wielded the stick - disobedience brings judgment: *"And it shall be, that just as the Lord rejoiced over you to do you good and multiply you, so the Lord will rejoice over you to destroy you and bring you to nothing; **and you shall be plucked from off the land which you go to possess.** Then the Lord will scatter you among all peoples, from one end of the earth to the other"* (Deut. 28:63-64). However, it is not as if the life and obedience demanded of Israel was onerous. The promise for obedience was not simply occupation of the designated territory, but blessing – blessing on the nation, blessing on families, blessing on crops. In addition, there would be protection from any nation that had ambitions to conquer. This was an agreement that was heavily weighted in favour of the nation. But sin makes a person foolish, and Israel played the fool with other gods that could neither bless nor protect. She reneged on her relationship with the LORD and was exiled as a result.

From our point in history we are very well aware of the periods of exile the Hebrew nation has suffered. The mass deportation of the ten tribes by Assyria was followed by the exile of the two tribes to Babylon. The most significant exile happened under the rule of the Romans, when Israel lost their Temple and their land for nearly two millennia. That was because they had rejected their Messiah. It was when the Babylonian exile was on the near horizon that Jeremiah prophesied of the New Covenant. The loss of Jerusalem, the Temple and the land was inevitable because, in his view, Israel no longer fulfilled their part of the Mosaic Covenant – the agreement had been broken by Israel,[106] and broken to such a degree that from that time forward it would never again function in the way it was intended.

It is true that there was a return after seventy years in Babylon, which might suggest that the nation had repented and re-embraced the Law of Moses, but Jeremiah rather suggests the return was the result of the Babylonians themselves coming under the rod of God. He predicted that after their seventy years of exile God would punish the Babylonians: *"'Then it will come to pass, when seventy years are completed, that I will punish the king of Babylon and that nation, the land of the Chaldeans, for their iniquity,' says the LORD; 'and I will make it a perpetual desolation.'"* (Jer. 25:12)

And the number of those that returned from Babylon to Jerusalem was very small – just a remnant of the two tribes that were taken there. Moreover, we have no evidence that any the ten tribes taken by Assyria returned. We will not underestimate the value of the believing remnant – but the Mosaic Covenant never resumed its rightful place in the life of the nation and consequently the nation has never since enjoyed a full, free and safe occupancy of the territory promised to Abraham and ruled over by David.

---

106   Jer. 31:32

Israel, the 'planting' of the LORD,[107] had been planted by God in a green and fertile environment, there to be tended by the great husbandman – a specialist with the highest qualifications. For it to be fruitful and multiply, the tender plant required protection and feeding. This the young nation received. Alas Biblical history suggests that when the divine husbandman went to harvest the crop all he found was wild grapes.[108] Such a disappointment!

However, this does not mean that the land element of the Abrahamic Covenant has been set aside. The land on the eastern shore of the Mediterranean is the legal inheritance of the Hebrew nation, and although they have been plucked from the land for unfaithfulness, there is yet predicted a time when they will occupy it in faith. Isaiah anticipated a time when Israel would return to God under the ministry of an anointed servant and occupy the land again. When he described the ministry of the Servant of the LORD; he wrote: *"The Spirit of the LORD GOD is upon Me, Because the LORD has anointed Me To preach good tidings to the poor; He has sent Me to heal the brokenhearted, To proclaim liberty to the captives, And the opening of the prison to those who are bound; To proclaim the acceptable year of the LORD, And the day of vengeance of our God; To comfort all who mourn, To console those who mourn in Zion, To give them beauty for ashes, The oil of joy for mourning, The garment of praise for the spirit of heaviness; That they may be called trees of righteousness, The planting of the LORD, that He may be glorified"* (Isa.61:1-3). If Israel repents *"… they shall rebuild the old ruins, They shall raise up the former desolations, And they shall repair the ruined cities, The desolations of many generations"* (Isa. 61:4). These early verses of Isaiah 61 were taken up by the anointed Servant of the LORD, Jesus of Nazareth, although He did indicate that His ministry then would only encompass the first one and a half verses. He read, *"The Spirit of the LORD is upon Me, because He hath anointed Me to preach the gospel to the poor; He hath sent me to heal the brokenhearted, to preach deliverance to the captives, and recovering of sight to the blind, to set at liberty them that*

---

107   Isa. 60:21
108   Isa. 5:2

are bruised, To preach the acceptable year of the Lord," for after that He closed the book. And only for the section that He read did He claim, *"This day is this scripture fulfilled in your ears"* (Luke 4:18-21, kjv). The remainder will have to wait for His return.

Chapter 9
The Davidic Covenant

The Abrahamic Covenant had promised a specific territory. Even though the victories of Joshua were outstanding, this covenant of grant was never fully realized in his time. The period between the death of Joshua and the rise of the monarchy was a period during which the tribes of Israel often forgot that they were a covenant people. The worship of the LORD frequently lapsed with the result that they were oppressed by the surrounding nations, often losing some of the territory that they had gained under Joshua. It was only after they repented did God raise up a charismatic leader to rally the people to arms and recover that which had been lost. These periods of relapse and recovery continued until a king was anointed to lead them. The occasion for it was a particularly heavy period of oppression. After some two hundred years of life in Canaan, the tribal confederacy was broken by the Philistines. Israel's army had been utterly defeated. Even the Ark, which they had taken into battle in the hope that it would turn the tide, was lost to the enemy. The priests that cared for it were slain. The Philistines then drove home their advantage by occupying as much of Israel's territory as they could. Having captured the Ark they then destroyed the Tabernacle at Shiloh. They placed garrisons at strategic locations. It was this particular oppression that led to the demand for a king. Saul, the king the people received, was commissioned to deliver Israel from the Philistine threat. Samuel was instructed, *"… you shall anoint him commander over My people Israel, that he may save My people from the hand of the Philistines"* (1 Sam. 9:16). But Saul did not complete his commission and although he had some initial victories he died at the hands of the Philistines. Israel was once again at their mercy.

It was at this time that David took hold of the remnant of Israel's army, and with inspired leadership and strategy, used them to propel Israel to be the dominant power in the area. His success was founded on his relationship with the covenant keeping God. When Saul was finally rejected for usurping the priest's office, Samuel informed him, "... *now your kingdom shall not continue. The Lord has sought for Himself a man after His own heart, and the Lord has commanded him to be commander over His people, because you have not kept what the Lord commanded you*" (1 Sam. 13:14). Not yet identified and anointed but described already as a man after God's own heart - this is some praise for a young man who, at that time, was looking after the family flock.

So David, with faith in the God of Israel, broke the power of the Philistines, drove them back to a narrow strip of land along the coast, and confined them there. They would never be a serious threat to Israel again. Indeed, Philistine soldiers were recruited as mercenaries in David's army. David also captured the Jebusite city of Jerusalem . He made it his capital, and completed the conquest of Canaan. Every inch of the land was now Israel or under Israelite domination. The influence that Israel exerted in that part of the Middle East was considerable. A new Israel had emerged.

Not only anointed by Samuel, but also anointed by the Spirit of God,[109] David had begun his career as a student in the school of the prophets, which had been established by Samuel at Naioth. Inspired by the Spirit of God, his musical gift was combined with a prophetic anointing to produce a number of Psalms for Israel's worship, some of which pointed forward to another anointed King who would yet reign over Israel.

At the height of his power he decided to bring the Ark to his capital city, Jerusalem.[110] It had lain neglected at Kirjath-Jearim. Initially, transporting it on a cart and incurring the displeasure of God, it was finally brought up to the city with an enormous military escort and great ceremony. Composing a Psalm

---

109   1 Sam. 16:13
110   2 Sam. 6

for the occasion[111] he organized the Levitical choir to pronounce that the 'King of Glory', 'the LORD of Hosts' was coming to Jerusalem to dwell. The Ark was His portable throne, and Jerusalem thus became the religious capital of Israel as well as its political centre. This would cement the newly established unity of the tribes around their new capital city and strengthen the throne. The affections of the people of Israel were now bound to Jerusalem in such a way that wherever they would be, and however far they travelled, they would always pray facing Jerusalem.

The establishing of the throne of David was clearly the will of the LORD because this kingdom would be a pointer to the Messianic kingdom which would grace Israel at a future date. The Tabernacle was erected on the Mount of Olives and the Ark housed there. But David's heart was still not satisfied. The tent-shrine needed to be replaced with something more permanent; perhaps a Temple where Israel could gather to fulfill their obligations at festival times. David voiced his thoughts to the prophet Nathan; *"See now, I dwell in a house of cedar, but the ark of God dwells inside tent curtains"* (2 Sam. 7:2). Initially, Nathan supported David's idea, but a message from the LORD, revised the program; *"Also the LORD tells you that He will make you a house. 'When your days are fulfilled and you rest with your fathers, I will set up your seed after you, who will come from your body, and I will establish his kingdom. He shall build a house for My name, and I will establish the throne of his kingdom forever. I will be his Father, and he shall be My son. If he commits iniquity, I will chasten him with the rod of men and with the blows of the sons of men. But My mercy shall not depart from him, as I took it from Saul, whom I removed from before you. And* **your house and your kingdom shall be established forever before you. Your throne shall be established forever'"** (2 Sam. 7:11-16, emphasis added).

The importance of this is evident in that the essence of it is repeated in the history recorded in first Chronicles: *"The LORD will build you a house. And it shall be, when your days are fulfilled, when you must go to be with your fathers, that I will set up your seed after you, who will be of your sons; and I will establish his kingdom.*

---

111   Ps. 24

He shall build Me a house, and I will establish his throne forever. I will be his Father, and he shall be My son; and I will not take My mercy away from him, as I took it from him who was before you. And I will establish him in My house and in My kingdom forever; and his throne shall be established forever" (1 Chron. 17:10-14).

Instead of David building a house for God, God would build a house for David, that is, God would establish David's dynasty. In the Samuel passage it speaks of Solomon inheriting the throne, but the historian who wrote Chronicles uses the word 'seed' in a similar fashion as it is used in the Abrahamic Covenant, allowing for the possibility that there will be a future son of David, apart from Solomon, who will build a house for the Lord, and who will hold the title 'Son of God', and who will reign eternally. Here is a promise of immense proportions; a promise of the Lord; a promise you can count on; a covenant promise! Any future Israelite who laid claim to the throne of the nation would have to come from the tribe of Judah and the line of David, although the sins of Jeconiah prevented any of his family from qualifying.[112]

Now although David himself was forbidden to build a Temple to house the Ark, this Covenant, the Davidic Covenant, purposed that his son Solomon, should fulfill David's ambition — *"He shall build Me a house"* (1 Chron. 17:12). It seems the desire of God to *"dwell among them"* (Ex. 25:8) was still in place. Certainly, when the Temple was completed and Solomon transferred the Ark to its new place of residence, the presence of God was evident, *"indeed it came to pass, when the trumpeters and singers were as one, to make one sound to be heard in praising and thanking the Lord, and when they lifted up their voice with the trumpets and cymbals and instruments of music, and praised the Lord, saying: "For He is good, For His mercy endures forever," that the house, the house of the Lord, was filled with a cloud, so that the priests could not continue ministering because of the cloud; for the glory of the Lord filled the house of God"* (2 Chron. 5:13-14).

---

112   Jer. 22:24-30

The Confirmation of the Covenant

Before David died he referred to the Covenant declaring that although he had not lived a blameless life, nevertheless the Covenant stood inviolate; *"He has made with me **an everlasting covenant**, Ordered in all things and **secure**"* (2 Sam. 23:5). Then again, the writer of Psalm 89 revels in the promises of God, especially those made to David; *"I will sing of the mercies of the LORD forever; With my mouth will I make known Your faithfulness to all generations. For I have said, 'Mercy shall be built up forever; Your faithfulness You shall establish in the very heavens.' 'I have made a covenant with My chosen, I have sworn to My servant David: 'Your seed I will establish forever, And build up your throne to all generations.'"* (Ps. 89:1-4)

Then again in vv. 34-37: *"**My covenant I will not break,** Nor alter the word that has gone out of My lips. Once I have sworn by My holiness; I will not lie to David: His seed shall endure forever, And his throne as the sun before Me; It shall be established forever like the moon, Even like the faithful witness in the sky."* [113]

Solomon succeeded David and the Temple was built on a sacred site in Jerusalem. By the time we come to the reign of Hezekiah the theology of the Davidic Covenant was well established. The covenant promise to David was then wider, larger and clearly indicated a future occupant of the throne who would own names that, in the Hebrew culture, transcend any that an earthly potentate might possess; *"For unto us a Child is born, Unto us a Son is given; And the government will be upon His shoulder. And His name will be called Wonderful, Counselor, Mighty God, Everlasting Father, Prince of Peace. Of the increase of His government and peace There will be no end, Upon the throne of David and over His kingdom, To order it and establish it with judgment and justice From that time forward, even forever. The zeal of the LORD of hosts will perform this"* (Isa. 9:6-7).

Jeremiah, who prophesied at a particularly difficult time, when the immediate future of Israel was under threat, had a further message. The terms of the Land Covenant were soon

---

113   See also Ps. 132:11 ff

to be invoked, and Israel would be exiled for disobedience and apostasy. It was at that time that he looked into the farther future and wrote: *"Behold, the days are coming," says the* LORD, *"That I will raise to David a Branch of righteousness; A King shall reign and prosper, And execute judgment and righteousness in the earth. In His days Judah will be saved, And Israel will dwell safely; Now this is His name by which He will be called: THE* LORD *OUR RIGHTEOUSNESS. "Therefore, behold, the days are coming," says the* LORD, *"that they shall no longer say, 'As the* LORD *lives who brought up the children of Israel from the land of Egypt,' but, 'As the* LORD *lives who brought up and led the descendants of the house of Israel from the north country and from all the countries where I had driven them.' And they shall dwell in their own land"* (Jer. 23:5-8).

Here he combined the two covenants, the Land Covenant and the Davidic Covenant, and while it is clear that the return from the Babylonian captivity is the immediate fulfillment of some of this prophecy, in common with many prophecies, it would need a further fulfillment in the farther future. The essence of this is repeated at 33:14-17. This prophet, much maligned by his contemporaries and facing the future with the knowledge that the power of the Davidic throne was to be broken by the Chaldean invaders, nevertheless had complete confidence in the covenant promise of God. He offered this assurance; *"Thus says the* LORD: *'If you can break My covenant with the day and My covenant with the night, so that there will not be day and night in their season, then My covenant may also be broken with David My servant, so that he shall not have a son to reign on his throne ...' Thus says the* LORD: *'If My covenant is not with day and night, and if I have not appointed the ordinances of heaven and earth, then I will cast away the descendants of Jacob and David My servant, so that I will not take any of his descendants to be rulers over the descendants of Abraham, Isaac, and Jacob. For I will cause their captives to return, and will have mercy on them'"* (Jer. 33:19-26).

While day and night remain, the Jewish nation is secure and the Covenant with David stands. Amos also gave the same assurance; *"On that day I will raise up the tabernacle of David, which has fallen down, And repair its damages; I will raise up its ruins, And rebuild it as in the days of old* (Amos 9:11).

Chapter 10
The Davidic Covenant - Its Purpose and Effect

There is nothing so comforting to us than knowing that we can lie down at night in security and peace, and then rise in the morning knowing that we will be safe to occupy ourselves with those activities in which we take pleasure. One of the great accomplishments of the reign of David was to bring about conditions that allowed that to happen in Israel. Solomon is known as the king of peace, but it is David, with God's help, that laid the foundation for it. The Psalmist captured the essence of this exactly; *"I will lift up my eyes to the mountains; From where shall my help come? My help comes from the Lord, Who made heaven and earth. He will not allow your foot to slip; He who keeps you will not slumber. Behold, He who keeps Israel will neither slumber nor sleep. The Lord is your keeper; The Lord is your shade on your right hand. The sun will not smite you by day, nor the moon by night. The Lord will protect you from all evil; He will keep your soul. The Lord will guard your going out and your coming in From this time forth and forever"* (Ps. 121:1-8).

If the kingdom of Israel, in the purposes of God, was to be a model, albeit a very limited model, of the future millennial kingdom, then there would be three areas in the domain of the king, which would need to function at a hundred percent efficiency – **warfare, welfare and worship**.

1. In Israel it was the king that had the responsibility of providing a blanket of security for his subjects. This could only be done with faith in God.

2. Furthermore, it would be he that would be required to look after the welfare of his people – that they had a comfortable existence living in a righteous and just society.

3. Moreover, he would have to ensure that the God of Abraham had His rightful place in their nation. Obedience to the law of Moses, and a functioning priesthood under the protection of the throne was essential.

These areas of responsibility are seen most clearly in the commissioning of the first three kings of Israel, the only kings that reigned over a united kingdom. However, the emphasis for each was different being dictated by the prevailing circumstances when they came to the throne. Saul was commissioned for **warfare** (to overcome the Philistines): *"I will send you a man from the land of Benjamin, and you shall anoint him commander over My people Israel, that he may* **save My people from the hand of the Philistines***; for I have looked upon My people, because their cry has come to Me."* (1 Sam. 9:16) Although he had some initial success, ultimately he failed due to disobedience. The Spirit of the LORD left him and the Philistines killed him.

David's fame in Israel was initially because of his success against their Philistine neighbors. He came to the public's attention when he slew Goliath. His victories as king included securing and fortifying the borders of Israel and maintaining a standing army. In this respect he laid the foundation for the halcyon days of peace that were enjoyed by Israel. He succeeded where Saul had failed; no doubt because his relationship with the LORD was stronger. But David was trained as a shepherd and as the shepherd king he was also required to look after the **welfare** of his people. A Psalm describes this aspect of his duties: *"He chose David also his servant, and took him from the sheepfolds; from following the ewes great with young he brought him to feed Jacob his people, and Israel his inheritance"* (Ps. 78:70-72). In addition, David, with a heart more in tune with God than any other king that would rise, gave due respect to the worship of the LORD. He reordered the priesthood into twenty-four courses; he composed Psalms, not only for his personal devotions but also for large Levitical choirs to sing; he brought the Ark to Jerusalem, and protected the Zadokian priesthood. In other words, David's claim to be Israel's greatest king is supported by his fulfilling his responsibility to care for the **welfare** and **worship** of his subjects after securing peace by successful **warfare**. Alas, there is no king that is without sin and even Israel's greatest earthly king, David, succumbed and the welfare of Israel was compromised. Adultery with Bathsheba and the murder of her husband, Uriah, led to civil war, and when he numbered Israel, 70,000 of his flock died.

Nevertheless, Solomon inherited a kingdom that was wealthy and secure. With the gift of wisdom from above, he entered on a reign of peace. His greatest contribution was in the area of **worship**. He fulfilled the commission passed to him by his father David[114] and replaced the tent-shrine of the LORD with a magnificent Temple that was graced by the divine presence at its dedication. But he too had feet of clay. Although he built the Temple, he failed to protect the worship of the God of Israel. He multiplied wives and with them idolatry. His activities led to the division the kingdom and therefore were the root cause of the northern kingdom setting up calf worship in Dan and Bethel. But he was the son of David and, because of that, a recipient of the '*chesed*' (loving-kindness) of God and secure in his position as king.

So the Davidic covenant is an acknowledgement that David was a man approved of God, who understood what was required of a king of Israel, and who sought to do it. He not only trusted God but was fully committed to Him. Consequently, he was God's choice to be the model for any who should reign over Israel. It is true that he sinned but when he did his repentance was full and sincere. God rewarded him with the promise of a dynasty and a name. But it would need a greater than David to provide for Israel real peace and security, guidance and sustenance, forgiveness and salvation. It would need great David's greater Son.

Summary

Saul was commissioned for warfare. He failed to do that for which he was chosen. Because of sin, the Spirit of the LORD left him and the Philistines killed him.

David came to the fore after the Spirit of the LORD came

---

114   2 Sam. 7:13

upon him at his anointing. He drove out the Philistines and succeeded in his military enterprises. He fulfilled a king's responsibility for **warfare**.

His added commission was to look after the welfare of his people, to lead them and to feed them. This he did and is known as the shepherd/king. But his record in respect of caring for the people is not without blemish. Because he committed adultery and murder, the displeasure of the LORD was incurred. The resultant civil war put Israelite against Israelite and when he numbered Israel 70,000 of his people died. While his record on **welfare** is reasonably good, it does have some serious blemishes.

In respect of **worship**, he cannot be surpassed. His prophetic and musical gifts come to the fore in the Psalms, and when he had a vision of Jerusalem being a Temple city, he was clearly expressing the mind of God. His was the vision, and his the preparations that made Solomon's Temple possible.

Solomon was a peaceful king. Because of David's success and legacy, he had no need to be a military king. But his record on welfare was not too good. His oppressive regime ultimately led to the division of the kingdom. And although he built the Temple, he failed to protect the worship of the LORD, and Israel was beset with idolatry until they returned from Babylon.

Of these three kings who reigned over a united Israel, it is David who was most able to fulfill the responsibilities of a king under God, and he is the one whose dynasty was established by covenant.

Chapter 11
The New Covenant

There is another covenant in the *T'nach*, the New Covenant. It was to be made with the nation of Israel. It is not a covenant that was in place in Jeremiah's time or applied to Jeremiah's generation, but it is Jeremiah who prophesied of the future when God would make this new covenant with the people of Israel. The detail is given in the 31st chapter of his prophecy: *"Behold, the days are coming, says the LORD, when I will make a new covenant with the house of Israel and with the house of Judah— not according to the covenant that I made with their fathers in the day that I took them by the hand to lead them out of the land of Egypt, My covenant which they broke, though I was a husband to them, says the LORD. But this is the covenant that I will make with the house of Israel after those days, says the LORD: I will put My law in their minds, and write it on their hearts; and I will be their God, and they shall be My people. No more shall every man teach his neighbor, and every man his brother, saying, 'Know the LORD,' for they all shall know Me, from the least of them to the greatest of them, says the LORD. For I will forgive their iniquity, and their sin I will remember no more"* (Jer. 31:31-34).

This text references two covenants - the Mosaic Covenant, the one which the Jewish nation had broken, and a New Covenant. The wording clearly establishes that the New Covenant, like the Mosaic Covenant, was to be made with the Jewish nation, identified as 'the house of Israel, and the house of Judah'. This was confirmed by Isaiah. He wrote: *"The Redeemer will come to Zion, And to those who turn from transgression in Jacob,"* Says the LORD. *"As for Me,"* says the LORD, *"this is My covenant with them: My Spirit who is upon you, and My words which I have put in your mouth, shall not depart from your mouth, nor from the mouth of your descendants, nor from the mouth of your descendants' descendants,"* says the LORD, *"from this time and forevermore"*(Isa. 59:20-21). That this Isaiah text refers to the New Covenant is confirmed in Paul's letter to the Romans, for he referenced the Isaiah quote when he wrote: *"And so all Israel will be saved, as it is written: 'The Deliverer will come out of Zion, And He will turn away ungodliness from Jacob; For this is My covenant with them, When I take away their sins'"* (Rom. 11:26-27).

These connected texts promise the regeneration of the Jewish nation under the implementation of a New Covenant, essentially because in it is the provision for the forgiveness of the sins of the nation, *"from the least of them to the greatest of them"*. This is a great improvement on the Mosaic Covenant; because that was only able to cover sins, not cleanse them. This aspect of the New Covenant is of the highest quality and the widest application.

In respect of the wideness of the application, there is a startling statement included in the Covenant, revealing that when the house of Israel and the house of Judah come into the full blessing of this Covenant, it will be a time when every member of the race will enjoy the fruits of salvation, for *"no more shall every man teach his neighbor, and every man his brother, saying, 'Know the LORD,' for they all shall know Me, from the least of them to the greatest of them, says the LORD. For I will forgive their iniquity, and their sin I will remember no more."* To put it a little more plainly, Jeremiah prophesied of a time that was still future to him when every member of the Jewish nation will have been saved.

That the blessing will be of the highest quality is evident for God declared, *"For I will forgive their iniquity, and their sin I will remember no more."* Their sins and iniquities will be forgiven and forgotten. Hallelujah!

While it is Jeremiah that provides the clearest description of the New Covenant, Isaiah had already indicated the blessing that it would bring to the Jewish people. He relayed the word of the LORD: *"For I, the LORD ... **will make with them an everlasting covenant**. Their descendants shall be known among the Gentiles, And their offspring among the people. All who see them shall acknowledge them, That they are the posterity whom the LORD has blessed."* (Isa. 61:8-9)

The quality of benefit that will be enjoyed by those that come under the New Covenant is described in terms of being indwelt by the Holy Spirit. Jeremiah quotes the LORD as saying, *"I will put My law in their minds, and write it on their hearts"*, and Ezekiel brings the message, *"**I will put My Spirit within you** and cause you to walk in My statutes, and you will be careful to observe My ordinances"* (Ezek. 36:27, emphasis added). Under the Mosaic economy the Spirit of the LORD came upon individuals for special and particular tasks. We have already remarked on the Spirit of the LORD leaving Saul and coming upon David. But the general population did not have that privilege. In this new dispensation, all of Israel, every individual Jew, will be indwelt by the Spirit of God. Joel, speaking of that day, uses the wide descriptor *"all flesh"* (Joel 2:28), that is, all Jewish flesh, without distinction and without exception. The failure to keep the Law will not arise; every Jew will be empowered to live righteously.

Ezekiel, who prophesied at a time when the Temple in Jerusalem had been destroyed, provides some further intelligence. Inasmuch as the future blessings for Israel were to be anchored on earth, with a return to the Land under a Davidic king in accordance with the two covenants that provided for those benefits, it seems right and proper that the greatest blessing that God could provide would be to dwell amongst them. The Mosaic Covenant provided for a Tabernacle *"that I may dwell among them"* (Exod.25.8). The Davidic Covenant provided for the Temple to be built.[115] The New Covenant will provide for the presence of God upon earth in a future Temple: *"Moreover I will make a covenant of peace with them, and it shall be an everlasting covenant with them; I will establish them and multiply them, and **I will set My sanctuary in their midst forevermore**. My tabernacle also shall be with them; indeed I will be their God, and they shall be My people* (Ezek. 37:26-27).

---

115   1 Chron. 17:12

Chapter 12
The New Covenant -
Its Purpose and Effect

The Jeremiah text implies it is a covenant that was designed to replace the Mosaic Covenant which was described as being 'broken'. The Jewish nation had been under the Mosaic economy for a considerable time, and no doubt could not envisage a day when the Law would not apply, but one fact is clear – because of the weakness of the flesh the dispensation of Law did not succeed in its main aim - to prepare the nation to receive her Messiah. That a conditional covenant should be replaced because one of the parties to the covenant could not fulfill her part of the contract is quite reasonable. Especially as it is to be replaced by a new covenant which essentially was unconditional, inasmuch as the terms laid down, placed the responsibility for the fulfilling of the covenant on one party only, and that was the party that had been faithful to the previous covenant. The LORD Himself would take responsibility to ensure Israel kept the Law by engraving its demands on the hearts of His people and then indwelling them Himself in the person of the Holy Spirit to provide the motivation, energy and ability to keep it. This is new for old, and the new is so much better, so much more comfortable, so much more fruitful, so much more God-glorifying and so much more satisfying.

The promise of this new covenant was a clear indication that God is faithful to His earlier promises for it envisages a time when the Abrahamic Covenant would be fulfilled in its entirety. The New Covenant gives an assurance to Israel that their future is safe in the hands of their God, that there is no way He has forgotten them and that they remain, as always, engraved on the palms of His hands.[116]

---

116   Isa. 49:15-16

The question naturally arises here – if the New Covenant is to replace the Mosaic Covenant because Israel had broken the conditions of the Covenant, what law is envisaged in these prophecies? YHWH described it as 'My law'; 'My statutes', 'My ordinances'. What laws, statutes and ordinances prevail under the New Covenant? They are best described as the laws of the Messiah. Jesus Himself described them as *"My commandments"* (John 14:15,21; 15:10,12). The motivation for keeping these commandments is love of the Saviour: *"If you love Me, keep My commandments"* (John 14:15). In this way the Jewish believer would reflect the attitude and relationship that exists between the Son of God and the Father: *"If you keep My commandments, you will abide in My love, just as I have kept My Father's commandments and abide in His love"* (John 15:10). And love is at the heart of the Messiah's law. *"A new commandment I give to you, **that you love one another; as I have loved you**, that you also love one another"* (John 13:34). It is a high standard – to love as Christ loves – but with His command He provides the enabling – the indwelling Holy Spirit: *"If you love Me, keep My commandments. And I will pray the Father, and He will give you another Helper, that He may abide with you forever"* (John 14:15-16). Again, *"If anyone loves Me, he will keep My word; and My Father will love him, and We will come to him and make Our home with him"* (John 14:23). This is part of the mechanics of the operation of the New Covenant, where He promised to put His law in Jewish hearts.

Chapter 13
The Messiah and the Covenants of Israel

Sinclair Patterson wrote: "Take away from Christianity the name and person of Jesus Christ and what have you left? Nothing! The whole substance and strength of the Christian faith centres in Jesus Christ. Without Him there is absolutely nothing."[117] This is also the case with the Covenants of Israel. Without the Messiah, there would be no true seed of Abraham through which the Abrahamic Covenant could be realized. Without the Messiah there would never be any single individual Israelite who could have fulfilled the Mosaic Covenant. Without the Messiah, the Land of Israel will never be fully recovered for the Hebrew nation. Without the Messiah there will never be a righteous reign by one of David's line, and without the Messiah there could never be a New Covenant providing forgiveness of sins and a new heart of obedience for the Jewish people.

Let us state clearly that the Covenants of Israel have held the nation together. Without the Covenants they could easily have lost their individual identity when dispersed among the other nations. It is the covenants that have molded their identity and been at the heart of their history. They have controlled its people and given them purpose. For them, they hold the revealed will of God - how they should act, where they should live, what their future is. They give the nation its purpose and form. They are glue that holds the Jewish race together. The substance and strength of Israel rest in their Covenants with God, and the Messiah is the substance and strength of the Covenants.

---

117   Sinclair Patterson. Quoted by Evans, W., & Coder, S. M. (1998, c1974). The great doctrines of the Bible. Includes index. (Enl. ed.) (53). Chicago: Moody Press.

Because the Covenants themselves are inter-twined and each one either progresses from the previous agreement or supplements it, it is difficult to consider them in isolation. Similarly, when we look at the relationship of the Messiah to the Covenants we will have difficulty in treating His relationship with each covenant separately, which means we will inevitably have to repeat some truths more than once when they apply in more than one instance.

Chapter 14
The Messiah and the Abrahamic Covenant

The Abrahamic Covenant was very wide ranging. Through Abraham it promised three main benefits – blessings (which must be assumed to be both spiritual and material), a multi-national posterity and a homeland for the Hebrew nation. All this was to be achieved through a 'seed', a line that would be fathered by Abraham and continue through his son Isaac and his grandson Jacob. The Land Covenant elucidated further the Jewish homeland element in the Abrahamic covenant (including the material blessings that would accrue to the inhabitants); the Davidic Covenant brought a further limiting element to the 'seed' aspect in conjunction with promising wide ranging influence; while the New Covenant identified the spiritual section of the blessings promised.

The Covenant Summarized

Any Messianic claimant would need to have the appropriate ancestry – of the seed of Abraham, Isaac, Jacob, of the tribe of Judah, of the family of David but not through Jeconiah.[118] Jesus of Nazareth, the Son of God and Israel's Messiah, had impeccable lineage. He was of the stock of Abraham, Isaac and Jacob, and the tribe of Judah. It is true that Joseph, the stepfather of Jesus, did come through the line of Jeconiah and was therefore disqualified, but he was not the father of the Messiah. Jesus was conceived of the Holy Spirit. This means that His birth fulfilled the most difficult and mysterious condition suggested by the *T'nach* – He was born of a virgin. In Genesis 3:15 the mysterious conqueror of Satan would be the 'seed of the woman'. Jesus, a true seed of the woman, qualified to fill that description. Moreover, Mary's lineage, which now becomes critical since she is His only earthly parent, is given in full in Luke's gospel, and satisfies every condition, even to being of the family of David without being tainted by the curse on Jeconiah's lineage. Although Isaiah had said centuries before the birth of Jesus, that a virgin would conceive, it is only in hindsight we are able to see that ultimately there was only one with the necessary qualifications to be the Messiah of Israel, that is, the Son of God who was conceived of the Holy Spirit, born of a virgin, and a true 'seed' of the woman. Jesus of Nazareth is the Immanuel[119] of Isaiah's prophecy, the 'Seed' of Abraham,[120] the 'Seed' and Son of David[121] and Son of God.[122]

There has never been any question that Jesus was a Jew, a true son of Abraham.[123] He was circumcised on the eighth day[124] and redeemed according to the Law.[125] Both his mother and step-father were Hebrews with a long and honourable lineage. In addition, His dress, His actions, His teaching, all testify to the thorough Jewishness of His person. He was law abiding in

---

119   Isa. 7:14 ; Matt. 1:23

120   Gal. 3:16; Heb. 2:16

121   Also called 'seed' in Acts 13:22-23; Rom 1:3; 1 Tim 2:8; but 'Son of David' in Matt. 1:1; 9:27; 12:23; 15:22; 20:30-31; 21:9,15; Mark 10:47-48; Luke 3:31; 18:38-39;

122   Matt. 8:29; 14:33; 27:54; Mark 1:1; 3:11; 15:39; Luke 1:35; 4:41; 8:28; John 1:34; 1:49; 3:18; 9:35-37; 11:27; 20:31; Acts 8:37; 9:20; Rom. 1:4; 2 Cor. 1:19; Eph. 4:13; Heb. 4:14; 1 John 4:15; 5:5,10; Rev. 2:18

123   Matt. 1:1

124   Luke 2:21

125   Luke 2:22

the sense that not only did He act in a responsible manner as a member of the community but He also did what was required to fulfill the Law of Moses. There are some Scriptures that teach us that He wore the appropriate clothes. In the episode where a woman needed a healing touch, she decided that if she could reach the hem of His garment she should be cured. The Greek word is 'kraspedon' sometimes translated 'fringe'. The Hebrew equivalent is 'zizith'. What is in view here are the fringes woven on to the outer garment that was worn by Jewish men. These fringes were four blue tassels worn in obedience to the injunction of the Law in Numbers 15:37–41 and Deuteronomy 22:12. Matthew again refers to them in 14:36 and 23:5. They consisted of four threads passing through the four corners of the garment and meeting in eight. One of the threads was longer than the others. It was twisted seven times round the others, and a double knot formed; then eight times, then eleven times, then thirteen times. The thread and the knots stood for the five books of the Law. The idea of the fringe was two-fold. It was meant to identify a Jew as a Jew and as a member of the chosen people, no matter where he was; and it was meant to remind a Jew every time he put on and took off his clothes that he belonged to God. Jesus had these fringes on His clothes.

We also know that He celebrated the feasts according to the instructions laid down in the *Pentateuch*. We have record of His visits to Jerusalem for Passover and the Feast of Unleavened Bread and we know He attended the Temple at the Feast of Tabernacles. Indeed, Jesus Himself said, *"Do not think that I came to destroy the Law or the Prophets. I did not come to destroy but to fulfill"* (Matt. 5:17). And that fulfillment was more than just being an obedient law abiding Jew - the will of God required Him to fulfill all that the Law required for the salvation of the Hebrew nation. This included all that the *Pentateuch* designated for the expiation and propitiation of sin; and all that was designated for the cleansing and purification of the sinner. Moreover, His death had to be accomplished in such a way that all prophecies and types laid down in the *T'nach*, which relate to the designated sacrifices, were satisfied perfectly. The designated sacrifices being – the Passover Lamb, the Lamb of the Sin Offering, the Offerings of the Day of Atonement and the Red Heifer, etc. When Jesus said it was laid on Him to 'fulfill the Law' 'fulfill' was used in its fullest sense.

So it was that Jesus was the 'fulfillment' of all that the Law was designed to accomplish. He was the only fully, Law abiding Hebrew that ever lived, and therefore the only One who could ultimately deliver the Jewish nation from the bondage of the Law.

There is a yet more vital element to this aspect of the proper lineage. Others also claimed to be descendents of Abraham but Jesus added yet one more qualification. Only those who did the will of God could be counted a true descendent of Abraham. John the Baptist implied it first. He said, *"do not think to say to yourselves, 'We have Abraham as our father.' For I say to you that God is able to raise up children to Abraham from these stones"* (Matt. 3:9; Luke 3:8). In other words, he indicated that the proper ancestry was insufficient in itself; they needed to be fulfilling the revealed will of God, which, for sinful members of the Hebrew race, was to repent and receive Jesus as their Messiah. The essence of this is repeated in the debate between Jesus and His Jewish listeners in John 8.38-45. But the will of God for the Messiah was to complete the mission for which He had been commissioned. This means that there could only have been one claimant to the title of Messiah, the One sent by the Father.

What is the sum of this? That if Jesus' claim to be the Messiah is to be upheld, He not only had to have the right lineage but also has be a faithful Son of Abraham and do the will of God. This He did. He said, *"I do not seek My own will but the will of the Father who sent Me"* (John 5:30), and, *"My food is to do the will of Him who sent Me, and to finish His work"* (John 4:34). That He was successful is evident. In His life He had the confirmation by the three Bat Kohls, the essence of which was, *"This is My beloved Son, in whom I am well pleased."* (Matt. 3:17; cf. 17:5; Mark 1:11; 9:7; Luke 3:22; 9:35; John 12:27-28). And after His death He had the vindication of the resurrection for it was God who raised Him from the dead.[126]

---

126   Acts 13:30, 34; 17:31; Rom. 10:9; Gal. 1:1; Eph. 1:20; Col. 2:12; 1 Pet. 1:21

Chapter 15

The Messiah and the Mosaic Covenant

When we considered the Mosaic Covenant we made some suggestions as to the purpose that God had in mind when He offered and signed it.[127] But that was an examination of the subject from an Old Testament viewpoint. Now we are in the dispensation of grace we must consider if we have more light on the subject. The answer is 'Yes.' If we ask, 'what was His purpose?' we have answers readily provided by the apostle Paul, a man personally instructed in the ways of God, for he asked and answered that very question.

"What purpose then does the law serve?" (Gal. 3:19). His immediate answer is in two parts. (1) It was added because of transgressions, and (2) till the Seed should come to whom the promise was made.

The Law was added because of transgressions

As the context in Galatians makes clear, the law Paul is referring to, is the Law of Moses, which was 'added' 430 years after the Abrahamic covenant. It was not added to alter the provisions of the Abrahamic covenant, but rather added in order to accomplish some supplementary purpose. This meaning is further clarified when we look at the parallel verse in Rom. 5:20: *"The law was added so that the trespass might increase."* In the Roman letter the word for 'added' (*pareisēlthen*) means literally "came in by a side road." The main road is the covenant of promise—inviolate, irrevocable. The law does not lead away from the main road, but leads back to it. It points to the same destination.

---

127   See chapter 6

The phrase, *"because of transgressions,"* can mean one of two things depending on whether the preposition *'charin'*, translated either "because," or "on account of," is given a causal (looking backward) or telic (looking forward) force. In the former case the Law would mainly have a preventive function. It this instance it would mean the Law was designed to curb or hold in check misdeeds that were already being done, in other words, to keep a bad situation from getting even worse. But if "because" is given a telic meaning, the opposite would hold true. The Law would have a provocative purpose, its function being not to prevent sins but actually to increase them, in other words, to make an already bad situation much, much worse.

The preventive and provocative functions correspond to the civil and spiritual uses of the law as developed by Luther. Luther suggested that God ordained civil laws for the purpose of restraining evildoers. Just as a rope or chain prevents a wild animal from attacking an innocent bystander, so too the law with its "thou shalt nots" and penal code prevents sinful humanity from going on a rampage and completely destroying itself. The civil use of the law helps to sustain human society. Luther referred to the state as the "left hand of God". But as important as the civil use of the law may be for the ordering of human society, it is at best a stopgap measure completely unable to render one righteous before God. The chief and proper use of the law, Luther said, is its provocative function, actually to increase transgressions, to make a terrible situation even more desperate, and thus to reveal to human beings their sin, blindness, misery, wickedness, ignorance, hate and contempt of God, which would ultimately lead to death, hell, judgement, and the well-deserved wrath of God. As Paul wrote, *"… by the law is the knowledge of sin"* (Rom. 3:20); it was added *"because of transgressions"* (Gal. 3:19).

The Law was added until the Seed should come

The second main reason that Paul identified, is its use to prepare the Israelite nation for their Messiah. Paul wrote – it was added until *"the Seed should come to whom the promise was made"* (Gal. 3:19).

Now the giving of the Law was strategically located at the birth of the nation - at the time when they enjoyed full freedom from slavery and when they had tasted the full effect of the power of God. They had been removed from the immediate influence of Egypt, especially the idolatry, and were, at that time, most open to new ideas. In other words, as a nation, they were in their infancy, and they could accept God as their Father. Indeed God said, *"Israel is My son, My firstborn"* (Ex. 4:22). And like an infant they had to trust God to feed them and to lead them. This idea of Israel being a nation in its infancy is very important. As such it was necessary for it to be placed under a tutor, and the Law is described as such, a schoolmaster that had been commissioned to fulfill one main purpose - to lead them to Christ, their Messiah, the 'Seed'. All activities, all lessons, all events, indeed the sum total of their education was to be directed to that purpose (Gal. 3:24).

Here is a nation that is to be trained. The whole penal, social and sacerdotal code was designed to impress upon them that (i) sin brings punishment; (ii) social injustice will not be tolerated (iii) but God is merciful and the mercy of God is always available. The calendar was so ordered that every member of every generation received full instruction on how to be a member of God's society. Moreover, if they learned their lessons well, they would be permitted to be instruments in God's hand, to demonstrate to the other nations of the world, the benefit of being subject to the rule of the beneficent God of Israel.

The Purpose of the Law (Diagrammatically)

The Giving of the Law – the Ethical and Moral standards expected also included instructions regarding

Tabernacle — Priesthood — Offerings — Festivals

All designed to lead them to their Messiah

The Mosaic code with its commandments and judgements was designed, among other things, to be a finger-post to point the nation of Israel to their Messiah. Since Israel was to be a theocracy, incorporated into the code were the regulations regarding worship. There were instructions for the erection of a sanctuary, the ordination of a priesthood, a description of the offerings they were to bring, and a diary of festivals that were to be celebrated when Israel was to come before the LORD and acknowledge His mercy and His grace. Besides the immediate purpose of regulating the worship of the individual Israelite and the nation as a whole, these also had another purpose. They too were to prepare them for their Messiah.

The Time Limit on the Law of Moses

If the Law was added until the seed came as Paul said, then this means that the Law had a limited duration. Just as it had a point of origin on Mount Sinai, so also it had a point of termination—Mount Calvary. 'Seed' is used as a name for Christ, echoing Paul's earlier identification: *"Now to Abraham and his Seed were the promises made. He does not say, 'And to seeds,' as of many, but as of one, **'And to your Seed,' who is Christ"** (Gal. 3:16, emphasis added). So the age of the Law is over. This truth is a part of Paul's theology. The texts, *"you are not under law"* (Rom. 6:14), and *"you ... have become dead to the law through the body of Christ"* (Rom. 7:4) encapsulate his teaching on the subject. School is out – Messiah has come – childish things are to be put away. What this means is: *"Christ is the end of the law for righteousness to everyone who believes"*. (Rom. 10:4) There was nothing wrong with the Law. The law was *"holy, and the commandment holy and just and good"* (Rom. 7:12). But salvation could not come by the Law, because no one could keep it.

Again, I repeat, the age of Law is over. So Paul interpreted the law eschatologically in terms of (i) its fulfillment and (ii) its cancellation, in the Messianic mission of Jesus. The Messiah *"wiped out the handwriting of requirements that was against us, which was contrary to us."* He took *"it out of the way, having nailed it to the cross"* (Col 2:14).

This section of Galatians is brim full of this idea that Christ's work on the cross brought an end to the Mosaic Law. Words like 'until'; 'before'; 'no longer'; 'formerly'; 'but now'. Things changed with the coming of the Messiah and His death by crucifixion. To repeat, *"Christ is the end of the law for righteousness to everyone who believes"* (Rom. 10:4).

We can now place the Mosaic covenant into our diagram.

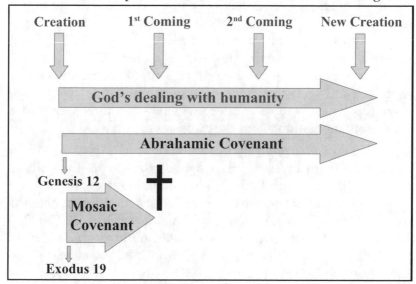

While the Abrahamic covenant is eternal, the Mosaic covenant was for a particular purpose and ceased when that purpose matured.

The inferiority of Law compared to Promise

We must also note that Paul added two further elements in explanation of the purpose of the Law, i.e. *"it was appointed through angels by the hand of a mediator"* (Gal. 3:19). This additional clause is designed to show the inherent inferiority of the law in terms of the way it was given and administered, that is, through angels and a mediator. Paul's meaning is clear: the law is not on the same par with the covenant of promise (that is, the Abrahamic covenant) not only because it was chronologically limited but also because it was handed down by angels with a

115

man acting as a go-between. The Hebrew text of Exodus chapter nineteen, which contains the scriptural account of the giving of the Law, does not refer to angels, but it does describe Mount Sinai as surrounded by thunder, lightening, a thick cloud, and billows of fire. (Ex. 19:16–19) Later Old Testament texts, notably the Septuagintal version of Deut. 33:2 and Psalm 68:18 interpret these natural phenomena to mean that a large number of angels, the fiery hosts of heaven, accompanied God in His giving of the law at Sinai. The participation of the angels in the giving of the law was not merely a piece of pious Jewish folklore, for it is confirmed elsewhere in the New Testament.[128] Paul accepted it and repeated it, not for the purpose of enhancing the law by associating it with the glory of angels, but rather to indicate how superior 'promise' is to 'Law' since the latter required a creaturely mediation.

The Law was not only mediated by angels but also Moses. The people themselves asked for a mediator. They said to Moses, you go to the Lord and relay to us what He says - we dare not come close. And in Pauline theology, Moses the mediator stands in contrast to Christ. As Paul explains more fully in 2 Cor. 3:7–18, the ministry or covenant negotiated by Moses was characterized by death and condemnation and it is *"fading away"*; on the other hand, the new covenant that Christ has ushered in is marked by life, justification, and a radiance *of "ever increasing glory, which comes from the Lord, who is the Spirit."*

Paul did not intend to denigrate Moses as a person but rather to show again the transitory and totally inadequate character of the Law as a system of salvation. The Epistle to the Hebrews picks up on one of Paul's favorite themes, that of servant and son, and applies them to Moses and Christ in precisely this way: *"Moses was faithful as a servant in all God's house ... but Christ is faithful as a Son over God's house"* (Heb 3:5–6;). But there is more: Paul gives another purpose to the giving of the Law. It is tied up with the phrase, *"it was added because of transgressions."* In other words, it was to bring the realization that sin was exceedingly sinful. Those that break God's law will suffer the curse. It

---

128   cf. Acts 7:38, 53; Heb. 2:2

was the case with Adam. He sinned and suffered the curse. But where there is no law there is no imputation of sin.[129]

By the Law comes the Curse

So the Law was brought in so that the curse could be pronounced on the law-breaker. In God's grace, under Law, He provided the sacrifices and priesthood to deal with any infractions committed. Nevertheless, *"For as many as are of the works of the law are under the curse; for it is written, 'Cursed is everyone who does not continue in all things which are written in the book of the law, to do them'"* (Gal. 3:10). The curse of the Law is more clearly defined in Deuteronomy 28, but see also Leviticus 26: *"But it shall come to pass, if you do not obey the voice of the LORD your God, to observe carefully all His commandments and His statutes which I command you today, that all these curses will come upon you and overtake you:*

"Cursed shall you be in the city, and cursed shall you be in the country.

"Cursed shall be your basket and your kneading bowl.

"Cursed shall be the fruit of your body and the produce of your land, the increase of your cattle and the offspring of your flocks.

"Cursed shall you be when you come in, and cursed shall you be when you go out" (Deut. 28:15-19).

From the application of these passages arose the practice of giving up habitual offenders to a *'cherem'* or curse. The Jews expressed it as giving them up to Satan. These obdurate law-breakers would lose the protection that God provided for His people. They would, like Job, be exposed to the activity of Satan, and could suffer a similar fate to Job. An offender who resisted correction and exhausted all remedy contained in the Law would become 'a curse among his people'. Jesus was brought face to face with some such individuals: a paralytic,[130] and a woman who washed His feet with her tears, (she is described as a sinner).[131] To both of these Jesus said, *"your sins are forgiven*

---

129   Rom. 5:13
130   Recorded in Matt. 9, Mark 2, and Luke 5
131   John 7:37 ff

you." The paralytic was also healed. A similar case to the para-lytic was the disabled woman who was bent over and could not stand up straight. The cause of this infirmity was identi-fied by the Messiah: "... *ought not this woman, being a daughter of Abraham, whom Satan has bound for eighteen years, be loosed from this bond on the Sabbath?"* (Luke 13.16). In forgiving their sins, healing their bodies and delivering them from Satan, Jesus was clearly anticipating the full benefit of His sacrificial death. This multi-layered act of redemption can only be explained by the fact that, among other things, they were delivered from the curse of the law.

But what happened at Calvary to make this sophisticated act of redemption possible? How were they, and indeed us, delivered from the curse of the Law? The answer is - by the act of substitution. Christ was pronounced *'cherem'* instead of us. Paul writes, *"Christ has redeemed us from the curse of the law, hav-ing become **a curse for us** (for it is written, 'Cursed is everyone who hangs on a tree')"* (Gal. 3:13, emphasis added).

The Crucified Christ deals with the curse of the Law

Here then is one reason why the death of the Messiah had to be by crucifixion. A 'cursed' Messiah, might be despised by the Jewish people but nevertheless was absolutely necessary for them. The Jewish people were under the 'curse of the Law' because they could not keep it. R. Levi said if they could only keep the Sabbath fully for one day, then Messiah would come.[132] But they could not perfectly keep the Law, even for only one day. The wider application of the curse also applies. The argument is, that if the Jews could not keep it, and they had every advantage, there is no way the Gentiles could have escaped the curse:*"Now we know that whatever the law says, it says to those who are under the law, that every mouth may be stopped, and **all the world may become guilty before God"*** (Rom. 3:19). Paul was very clear. He said that returning to the Mosaic covenant only led to bondage, the curse and death: *"For as many as are of the works of the law are under the curse; for it is written, 'Cursed is everyone who does not*

---

132   Midrash Rabbah on Ps. 95:7

continue in all things which are written in the book of the law, to do them'" (Gal. 3:10 cf. Deut. 27:26). No-one is justified by the Law,[133] for *"there is none righteous, no not one"* (Rom. 3:10).

A Proper Appreciation of the Law would lead to an appreciation of the Messiah

So, in the letter to the Galatians he spelt out the purpose of the Law. It was a schoolmaster to lead the Jewish people to their Messiah.[134] If the Jewish people had accepted their Messiah, they would have had a graduation ceremony. Then, no longer under the tutorship of the Law, they could have enjoyed all the privileges and responsibilities of sons of God, as Paul indicated: *"But when the fullness of the time had come, God sent forth His Son, born of a woman, born under the law, to redeem those who were under the law, that we might receive the adoption as sons"* (Gal. 4:4-5). They would have entered into that condition of grace that the Church now enjoys, for *we "are not under law but under grace"* (Rom. 6:14). Alas, the leadership of the nation failed their finals. The Law had given the Sanhedrists power over the people and they did not want to relinquish it. Moreover they considered themselves patriotic Jews by defending not only the Mosaic Law but also the extrapolated laws of the teachers, now preserved for us in the Mishnah. They even accused the Messiah of breaking the law, He who had come to fulfill the Law and redeem them from the Law. But God is very gracious. Although nationally, because of the failure of their ruling body, the Jews did not pass their exams, the grace of God made it possible for individuals to graduate. Peter exhorted all who heard him to separate themselves from the national decision taken by the Sanhedrin. Then they could be saved. Saul, the Pharisee, (in some ways a special case) graduated in the school of the Messiah. Moreover, he gave private tutorials and led others to faith in *Yeshua HaMashiac* (Jesus the Messiah). Believers said of him, he is preaching the *"faith which he once tried to destroy"* (Gal. 1:23). So Rabbi Saul, champion of Law and works, as he testified: *"And I advanced in Judaism beyond*

---

133   Gal. 2:16
134   Gal. 3:24

many of my contemporaries in my own nation, being more exceedingly zealous for the traditions of my fathers" (Gal. 1:14), became the Apostle Paul, champion of grace and faith: *"For by grace you have been saved through faith, and that not of yourselves; it is the gift of God"* (Eph. 2:8).

Furthermore, in his letter to the Galatians he urged the readers to *"Stand fast therefore in the liberty by which Christ has made us free, and do not be entangled again with a yoke of bondage"* (Gal. 5:1). To paraphrase his argument—now that you have been saved by grace, do not think that you remain a child of God by works. That path makes the cross of Christ of no effect. By the time we come to his letter to the Colossians, his theology of the crucified Messiah is more mature. There he declared that the Messiah dealt a fatal blow to the Law: *"Blotting out the handwriting of ordinances that was against us, which was contrary to us, and took it out of the way"* (Col. 2:14). So, for those who have put their faith in a crucified Messiah, the curse of the Law is negated by the action of the cross.

Anne Ross Cousin wrote

> Death and the curse were in our cup,
>
> O Christ, 'twas full for Thee!
>
> But Thou hast drained the last dark drop,
>
> 'Tis empty now for me.
>
> The bitter cup, love drank it up;
>
> Now blessings' draught for me.

To Summarize

The Law was given:
- to provide an ethical, moral and social structure to Israel as a nation.
- to emphasize the righteousness of God and the sinfulness of man.
- to demonstrate the grace and mercy of God (through the sacrificial system).

- to lead them to recognize the grace and mercy of God when the Son of God came as their Redeemer and sin bearer.

However, the Law is now no longer the pattern for righteous living. For that we need to look to the Messiah, who not only fulfilled the Law but also died to remove the curse of the Law.

Chapter 16
The Messiah and the Land Covenant

The Land Covenant made the occupation of Israel conditional on the obedience of the people to the Mosaic Law. One of the purposes of the Mosaic Law was to prepare Israel to receive their Messiah. Jesus said, *"If you believed Moses, you would believe Me; for he wrote about Me"* (John 5:46). The rejection of the Messianic claims of Jesus is a prima facie case against Israel that they were not keeping the Law. This is also the direct accusation of the Son of God, the only One who never told a lie: *"Did not Moses give you the law, **yet none of you keeps the law?**"* (John 7:19), immediately adding, *"Why do you seek to kill Me?"* thus identifying the final act of His rejection, which, if the Word of God holds true would have to bring about an exile of the nation. And so it was. The Messiah who never shed tears over His own pain shed tears over the judgement that was to fall on Jerusalem. When He saw the city He wept over it, saying, *"If you had known, even you, especially in this your day, the things that make for your peace! But now they are hidden from your eyes. For days will come upon you when your enemies will build an embankment around you, surround you and close you in on every side, and level you, and your children within you, to the ground; and they will not leave in you one stone upon another, because you did not know the time of your visitation"* (Luke 19:41-44).

Jesus indicated that the exile would not really end until they reversed the national rejection of His Messianic office: *"O Jerusalem, Jerusalem, the one who kills the prophets and stones those who are sent to her! How often I wanted to gather your children together, as a hen gathers her chicks under her wings, but you were not willing! See! **Your house is left to you desolate;** for I say to you, **you shall see Me no more till you say, 'Blessed is He who comes** *in the name of the Lord!'"* (Matt. 23:37-39; Luke 13.34). The desolation of Israel will not end until they repent of national rejection of the Son of God, and call for His help and assistance. Israel cannot survive without God, and it is only the believing remnant that maintains the continuity of their existence.

On the way to His place of execution, when His rejection would be finally confirmed by the most unjust and cruel act imaginable, He repeated His warning to the nation. In view of their statement, *"His blood be on us and on our children"* (Matt. 27:25), Jesus said, *"Daughters of Jerusalem, do not weep for Me, but* **weep for yourselves and for your children.** *For indeed the days are coming in which they will say, 'Blessed are the barren, wombs that never bore, and breasts which never nursed!' Then they will begin 'to say to the mountains, "Fall on us!" and to the hills, "Cover us!"' For if they do these things in the green wood, what will be done in the dry?"* (Luke 23:28-31, emphasis added).

The leaders of the nation, supported by the majority of the population, had rejected their Messiah with the words, *"Away with Him, away with Him! Crucify Him! ... We have no king but Caesar!"* (John 19:15). They will find out what kind of king Caesar is. Not insignificantly, Caesar also claimed the honour of being a deity.

The physical consequences of the rejection of Jesus and the fulfillment of His chilling prophecy to the women of Jerusalem did not mature until more than three decades later. Gessius Florus, the Roman governor/procurator of Israel from AD 64 to 66 was not averse to utilizing his power for personal gain. Josephus blames him for 'kindling the war',[135] that is, it was Florus' actions that brought about the Jewish revolt that ultimately led to the fall of Jerusalem and the destruction of the Temple. Several Roman commanders were involved. The campaign was begun by the governor of Syria, Cestius Gallus, who, with the 12th legion, plus two thousand men from other legions and reinforced with cavalry and auxiliary troops, began the campaign to subdue a revolt by the disenchanted Jewish people. His campaign began successfully enough but he failed

---

135   The works of Josephus, Wars 2, 556

to take the Temple Mount and withdrew. Gallus was succeeded by Vespasian and Vespasian's son, Titus, and it would be Titus who would finally conquer Jerusalem, over-run the opposition on the Temple Mount and destroy the Temple. The Titus arch, erected in Rome to memorialize his victory, depicts the seven branch Menorah being carried away by Roman legionaries.

Although the Jews were seriously depleted and some exiled at the time of the Vespasian war, it would be the rebellion under the Messianic claimant Bar Cochba that would bring about the wholesale deportation of the population. In AD 132 Simon Bar Cochba persuaded many leading Jews that he was the Messiah and would be able to lead a resistance against Rome that would be the fulfillment of the word of the prophets and free them from the Gentile yoke. Initially there was some success, but Rome always had reinforcements and the ability to put down rebellions, and the revolt was finally subdued in AD 135. However, the cost to Rome was heavy, both in the loss of men and resources. The province itself was reduced to a wilderness. Schurer reports "All Judea was well-nigh a desert. 50 fortresses, 985 villages were destroyed, 580,000 Jews (?) fell in battle, while the number of those who succumbed to their wounds and to famine was never reckoned. Innumerable was the multitude of those who were sold away as slaves. At the annual market at the Terebinth of Hebron they were offered for sale in such numbers that a Jewish slave was of no more value than a horse. What could not be disposed of there was brought to Gaza and there sold or sent to Egypt, on the way to which many died of hunger or by shipwreck."[136] Jerusalem was converted into a Roman colony with the name Aelia Capitolina. The character of the city was transformed from Jewish to heathen by driving out any remaining Jewish occupants, and replacing them with colonists. No Jew was allowed to re-enter the city. Any discovered within its boundaries was put to death. A Temple to Jupiter was erected to replace the Jewish Temple on the Temple mount. That

---

136   Schürer, E. (1890). A history of the Jewish people in the time of Jesus Christ, first division, Vol. II. (Edinburgh: T&T Clark.)(2:314).

which Antiochus Epiphanes had tried to accomplish some centuries earlier was now accomplished by the Roman conquerors. Thus the Jews finally and completely lost the Temple, the City and the Land. It would be some 1800 years before they would have a partial foothold in Israel once again.

The Return of the Jews to the Land

The obedience to the Law that was required was always predicated on faith. Mechanical obedience was never acceptable to the LORD. Not unsurprisingly, their historical obedience was never perfect and when the quality of that obedience dropped to unacceptable levels there would be a word from the throne via a prophetic spokesman to indicate an exile of the people. An examination of texts in the *T'nach* suggests there would be at least three dispossessions[137] and three restorations.[138] Of those, the three dispossessions have been fulfilled, so also the first and second restorations; the final restoration for which the nation waits is yet future.

Since the final return to the Land is conditioned on faith in God, then it will only take place when the nation accepts Jesus as their Messiah and are regenerated. It is true that there has been a return to the Land in the 20th century, but the numbers have been relatively small, and the bulk of the population have returned in unbelief, that is, they are still not followers of Jesus, the Messiah of Israel. Therefore, they do not qualify for the full restoration of the Land. This waits for the nation as a whole to repent, embrace God's offer of mercy, and enjoy the benefits that the New Covenant can bring to them. Only then will they occupy the territory designated in the Abrahamic Covenant which at that time will be restored to full fruitfulness.

---

137   cf. Gen. 15:13-14,16; Jer. 25:11-12; Deut. 28:63-68 with Deut. 30:1-3

138   cf. Gen. 15:14 with Josh. 1:2-7; Dan.9:2 with Jer. 25:11-12; Deut. 30:3; Jer. 23:5-8; Exek. 37:21-25; Acts 15.14-17

Here are a few Scriptures relating to this:

1. **The final regathering will be when Israel returns in faith**. Moses spoke of it: *"But if they confess their iniquity and the iniquity of their fathers, with their unfaithfulness in which they were unfaithful to Me, and that they also have walked contrary to Me … then I will remember My covenant with Jacob, and My covenant with Isaac and My covenant with Abraham I will remember; I will remember the land …when they are in the land of their enemies, I will not cast them away, nor shall I abhor them, to utterly destroy them and break My covenant with them; for I am the Lord their God. But for their sake I will remember the covenant of their ancestors, whom I brought out of the land of Egypt in the sight of the nations, that I might be their God: I am the Lord"* (Lev. 26:40-45).

2. **It will be a total regathering.** Isaiah described it: *"Fear not, for I am with you; I will bring your descendants from the east, And gather you from the west; I will say to the north, 'Give them up!' And to the south, 'Do not keep them back!' Bring My sons from afar, And My daughters from the ends of the earth— Everyone who is called by My name, Whom I have created for My glory; I have formed him, yes, I have made him"* (Isa. 43:5-7).

3. **The Land will be restored to its former glory**. *"'I will bring back the captives of My people Israel; They shall build the waste cities and inhabit them; They shall plant vineyards and drink wine from them; They shall also make gardens and eat fruit from them. I will plant them in their land, And no longer shall they be pulled up From the land I have given them,' Says the Lord your God"* (Amos 9:14-15).

4. **God will be a shepherd to Israel**. *"'Hear the word of the Lord, O nations, And declare it in the isles afar off, and say, 'He who scattered Israel will gather him, And keep him as a shepherd does his flock'"* (Jer. 31:10).

Chapter 17
The Messiah and the Davidic Covenant

The Davidic Covenant promised:

1. An eternal house (this refers to the dynasty of David; the house of David or the line of David).

2. An eternal throne (this refers to a permanent right to reign that was to be held by the house of David).

3. An eternal kingdom (Israel's future is secure - there will always be subjects to protect and serve).

4. An eternal descendent (necessary if the house, throne and kingdom are to last forever).

That the Davidic Covenant climaxes in the person of the Messiah is supported by Scripture. Peter references it in his address at Pentecost: *"Men and brethren, let me speak freely to you of the patriarch David, that he is both dead and buried, and his tomb is with us to this day. Therefore, being a prophet, and knowing that God had sworn with an oath to him that of the fruit of his body, according to the flesh, He would raise up the Christ to sit on his throne, he, foreseeing this, spoke concerning the resurrection of the Christ, that His soul was not left in Hades, nor did His flesh see corruption"* (Acts 2:29-31). Here is the eternal One, resurrected to sit eternally on the Davidic throne.

In this address Peter draws on Psalm 16 to demonstrate that the resurrection of Jesus was predicted, and since the Psalm was Davidic it must mean that this One who has been resurrected, the Messiah of Israel, must also be the One to inherit the throne of David and reign eternally. Peter builds his case quickly and well. Since he was speaking on the anniversary of the death of David, and because the tomb of David was known to his hearers, he confidently asserted that Israel's greatest king was both dead and buried. The unexpressed implication is that since David's tomb remains undisturbed, his body underwent decay, so he cannot have fulfilled the prophecy spoken of in Psalm 16. And if David cannot fulfill the psalm, someone else must. Peter offers the solution in verse 30. Knowing that God had promised to seat one of his descendants on his throne, David spoke prophetically of the resurrection of the Messiah. With this statement, Peter interpreted Psalm 16 in light of God's promise to David. The resurrection, and (by implication) the death of the Messiah, was predicted in this Psalm (vv. 8–11) and are part of the fulfillment of the promise to seat one of David's descendants on his throne. While the promise statement in verse 30 of Acts 2 is an allusion from the Septuagint translation of Psalm 132:11, it surely draws generally from the Davidic theology that most Jews would have been familiar with.[139]

A later episode is described in Acts 15. There Luke undertakes to report on the debate in Jerusalem, where the question of the admittance of the Gentiles was under discussion. He quotes James quoting Amos: *"After this I will return And will rebuild the tabernacle of David, which has fallen down; I will rebuild its ruins, And I will set it up; So that the rest of mankind may seek the LORD, Even all the Gentiles who are called by My name, Says the LORD WHO DOES ALL THESE THINGS"* (Acts 15:14-17; cf. Amos 9:11-12). The prophecy of the rebuilding of the tabernacle (or house) of David again draws on the promise to David that his house, throne and kingdom would be established forever.[140] It appears that the early Church leaders understood the rebuilding of David's house in this way—as a reference to the re-establishment of the Davidic dynasty accomplished through the death, resurrection and exaltation of Jesus.

Not only 'Son of David' but also 'King of the Jews'

It was crucial to the Messianic claim of Jesus that He should have been born in David's town of Bethlehem, of David's

---

139 Cf. 2 Sam. 7:12–16; Ps. 89
140 cf. 2 Sam. 7:16

line and be a true Son of David, a title that was freely accorded Him by those who recognized His Messianic credentials.[141] But beyond this is His position as 'King of the Jews'. He was not just of royal lineage, (many others could have claimed as much), but He was the only One who would be able to fulfill the royal prophecies. He was born *"King of the Jews"* (Matt. 2:2); He was tried as *"King of the Jews"* (Matt. 27:11; John 18:33), a title he readily accepted before Pilate,[142] a title that Pilate readily accepted;[143] and He was convicted and executed as *"King of the Jews"* (Matt. 27:37; Mark 15:26; Luke 23:38; John 19:19).

At the centre of the rejection of Jesus as Messiah was the reluctance of the Sanhedrin to acknowledge this aspect of the claim of Jesus. When He entered Jerusalem riding on a donkey, deliberately fulfilling the Zechariah prophecy, *"Tell the daughter of Zion, 'Behold, **your King is coming to you**, Lowly, and sitting on a donkey, A colt, the foal of a donkey'"* (Matt. 21:4-5), they complained of the crowd's reaction when they praised the Son of David. This public display of power and popularity undoubtedly hardened their opposition and resistance. Their actions the following week where they sought opportunity to bring a political accusation against Him were partly a reaction to this event.

That Jesus had title to the Davidic throne is clear, but the time when His reign would begin is less clear. The disciples had thought it was imminent. After the resurrection and before the ascension they asked the risen Messiah, *"LORD, will You at this time restore the kingdom to Israel?"* (Acts 1:6). Jesus' enigmatic reply was, *"It is not for you to know times or seasons which the Father has put in His own authority."* (Acts 1:7) It seems obvious that there will be no salvation for the nation of Israel until they acknowledge, not just the Messianic claim of Jesus, but also His Davidic claim. When He returns, He will return as King, and not just King of the Gentiles but especially King of the Jews. And He will reign from Jerusalem. Therefore it must await the

---

141   Matt. 9:27; 12:23; 15:22; 20:30-31; 21:9; Mark 10:47-48; 18:38-39 (see also Matt.1:1; Luke 3:31)

142   Matt. 27:11

143   Mark 15:9

time when the leaders will greet the Messiah in the same manner as the crowd did at His entry into Jerusalem on the first day of Passion week. They are required to express heartfelt delight at His appearing, fulfilling the main condition for His return; *"...you shall see Me no more till you say, 'Blessed is He who comes in the name of the LORD!'"* (Matt. 23:39).

Chapter 18
The Messiah and the New Covenant

That the death of the Messiah provided the basis and ground for the implementation of the New Covenant can be ascertained from the events that took place the night before His execution. In conformity to the historic command of Moses to celebrate the Passover on the 14th of Abib (Nisan); He hosted the remembrance meal for His disciples. The table was furnished with the roast meat of a lamb that had been killed in the Temple, and every aspect of the celebration had been meticulously followed, including the provision of unleavened bread and wine. They had drunk from the cup of thanksgiving, and eaten of the bitter herbs, dipping them in salt water, and haroset. They had feasted on the lamb, reclining at table as free men. It was when they were due to drink the third cup of wine, the cup of blessing, that the Messiah introduced a new aspect to the festival. Taking some of the unleavened bread He *"gave thanks and broke it, and gave it to them, saying, 'This is My body which is given for you; do this in remembrance of Me'"* (Luke 22:19). In a similar fashion *"He also took the cup after supper, saying, 'This cup is the new covenant in My blood, which is shed for you'"* (Luke 22:20; see also Matt. 26:28; Mark 14:24; 1 Cor. 11:25). In anticipation of His execution the following morning, He informed the future leaders of the Church that His death was ground for the commencement of a new dispensation, a dispensation of grace, a dispensation that would be founded on the New Covenant. It is His death that permits the implementation of that aspect of the New Covenant that grants forgiveness for sin. And it is His resurrection that points to the implementation of the Davidic Covenant, and it is His ascension that furnishes the Holy Spirit to indwell His followers.

But how can we explain the implementation of the New Covenant as it was practiced in the early Church, for it stands in contrast to the Jeremiah text which points it directly to the houses of Judah and Israel and clearly anticipates it being activated for the nation as a whole? Paul, a minister of the New Covenant[144] and apostle of the Messiah with a special remit to go to the Gentiles, offered to them the benefits of the New Covenant without requiring their conversion to Judaism. Moreover, the book of Hebrews spends a great deal of time developing the argument that the New Covenant, that had been activated by the death, resurrection and ascension of the Messiah, is substantially better that anything provided in the Mosaic Covenant.[145] On the face of it this does not present any problem, but in light of the Jeremiah prophecy, it is slightly off centre because the Hebrew letter is directed, not to the nation as a whole but to those who have individually recognized the Messianic claims of Jesus of Nazareth.

The foundation text in Jeremiah[146] speaks of the New Covenant being activated for the nation as a whole, but in the early Church it was activated for individual Jews as well as individual Gentiles.

How so? Let's find answers to this conundrum.

---

144   2 Cor. 3:6
145   See Heb. 7:22; 8:6-13; 9:15; 10:16,29; 12:24; 13:20
146   Jer. 31:31-34

Chapter 19
The Church and the New Covenant

The New Covenant as it applies to Individual Members of the Hebrew Race

For what has been observed so far it seems that the implementation of the New Covenant for the Hebrew nation as a whole awaits a future day when they will be brought to acknowledge Jesus as Messiah and King. How can it be implemented for individuals? It is Peter that began the process. This was to be expected – for he had been specially selected for that ministry. The record of his commissioning is in Matthew chapter 16. It took place when Peter himself was finally and completely convinced of the Messianic claims of Jesus. He confessed, *"You are the Christ (the Messiah), the Son of the living God"* (Matt. 16:16). These titles encompass the person and work of the incarnate God. Jesus indicated this was to be the foundation for a new order, a collective of people with the same conviction, that Jesus is both Messiah and Son of God: *"Blessed are you, Simon Bar-Jonah, for flesh and blood has not revealed this to you, but My Father who is in heaven. And I also say to you that you are Peter, and on this rock I will build My church, and the gates of Hades shall not prevail against it. And I will give you the keys of the kingdom of heaven, and whatever you bind on earth will be bound in heaven, and whatever you loose on earth will be loosed in heaven"* (Matt. 16:17-19).

Those that have the same conviction and confession as Peter will be called out to be a new entity, the *'ekklesia'*, the called out ones, the Church. Since the *'ekklesia'*, the Church, is here spoken of as a building, the analogy is continued by the use of the image of 'keys.' Peter is considered to be the steward with the keys to the building. His ministry, recorded by Luke in the book of Acts, includes those occasions when he opened the door to the kingdom of heaven and admitted Messianic believers into the Church.

The Introduction of the new 'house rules' that controlled entry and membership of the Church.

To facilitate this change to the implementation of the New Covenant, Peter is given authority to bind and loose. Within Jewish culture these words are understood to mean forbid and permit. The terms *binding* and *loosing* were in regular use in rabbinic canon-law. They represented the *legislative* and *judicial* powers of the rabbinic office. In the new age that was dawning, that is, the Church age, these powers were granted by the head of the Church, the Messiah, first to Peter, and later to the other apostles.[147] These were the ones charged to advertise the new 'house rules' that were to be in place in the new dispensation of grace. Holders of the apostolic office were empowered to immediately offer the benefits of the New Covenant to those individuals who qualified to enter the Church, that is, those individuals whose confession of Jesus is that He is the Messiah, the Son of God. Once the door had been opened, of course, others were permitted to enter, as long as it was on the same basis – acceptance of the person and work of the Messiah.

The Day of Pentecost

Those believers that qualified to be members of the new order, the Church, were gathered in Jerusalem at the Feast of Weeks, when the ascended Son of God sent the Spirit of God to initiate the New Covenant for them. As with the Messiah at His baptism, so now with the disciples of the Messiah, the Spirit of God descended and rested upon each of them. More than that, He indwelt them, thus fulfilling that part of the New Covenant that speaks of the law, statutes and ordinances of God being written on tablets of flesh. Spontaneous praise to God broke out and was heard and understood by many of those who were in Jerusalem for the feast, no matter which was their native

---

147   John 20:23

language. This phenomenon drew much public attention, and gave Peter an opportunity to explain the significance of these unusual events and how they were the activity of the Man that was recently crucified, but who had been resurrected and returned to heaven to a place of honour at the throne above. In this, the first public address of the new dispensation, Peter references prophetic Scriptures to explain what had happened. He brought forward the words of Joel who spoke of the day when the New Covenant would be in play. Peter said, "… *this is what was spoken by the prophet Joel: 'And it shall come to pass in the last days, says God, That I will pour out of My Spirit on all flesh; Your sons and your daughters shall prophesy, Your young men shall see visions, Your old men shall dream dreams. And on My menservants and on My maidservants I will pour out My Spirit in those days; And they shall prophesy'*" (Acts 2:16-18). That Joel was speaking of a day when the Spirit of God will be poured out upon all flesh, that is all Jewish flesh, is supported by other writers. For example, Paul says, "*all Israel will be saved, as it is written: 'The Deliverer will come out of Zion, And He will turn away ungodliness from Jacob'*" (Rom. 11:26). In that future day it will be all Jewish flesh without exception. But the *T'nach* regularly uses the words 'all flesh' to refer to the whole of humanity.[148] And, in the light of the historic events of the day of Pentecost, we must initially interpret the phrase as all flesh without distinction, that is, the young and the old, male and female, bond and free. And later events allow us to add Jew and Gentile but that is getting ahead of ourselves.

Many of the crowd convicted by Peter's words, no doubt because they had tacitly, if not actively, rejected the claims of Jesus, raised the question, "*what shall we do?*" (Acts 2:37). This prompted Peter, apostle to the Jews, and holder of the keys of the kingdom of heaven, to respond and in his response we will find the clue needed to illuminate how it would be possible for individual Jews to receive the blessings of the New Covenant. Peter said, "*'Repent, and let every one of you be baptized in the name of Jesus Christ for the remission of sins; and you shall receive the gift*

---

148   Gen. 6:12-13,17; Job 34:15; Ps. 65:2; 145:21; Isa. 40:5-6, etc

of the Holy Spirit. For the promise is to you and to your children, and to all who are afar off, as many as the LORD *our God will call.' And with many other words he testified and exhorted them, saying, 'Be saved from this perverse generation'"* (Acts 2:38-40, emphasis added). What is envisaged here is an offer of the blessing of the New Covenant to those who would distance themselves from the decision of the nation's leaders and recognize Jesus as Israel's Messiah and take Him as their LORD. Peter, in saying, *"Be saved from this perverse generation"* recognized that it was 'this generation' that was under a suspended sentence from the Son of God. Those that wish to be saved from the blanket judgment that was upon the nation were required to act then, on the day of Pentecost, in the same manner as the whole nation will be required to act sometime in the future. Indeed, any Israelite of any generation has the same opportunity, and can know the same salvation, if they fulfill the conditions that Peter laid on his listeners, to recognize Jesus as Messiah and LORD.

The Messiah and 'This Generation'

The Messiah, who always chose His words with great care, isolated His contemporary generation from all other generations when He spoke of His rejection. *"...He (the Son of Man) must suffer many things and be **rejected by this generation**."* (Luke 17:25, emphasis added) It will be that single generation that will stand at the bar of God and be accused of unlawfully rejecting their Messiah, because it was with that one generation He contended. He never said 'all future generations' will be under the judgment of God; He only ever said, 'this generation.' *"The men of Nineveh will rise up in the judgment with **this generation** and condemn it, because they repented at the preaching of Jonah; and indeed a greater than Jonah is here. The queen of the South will rise up in the judgment with **this generation** and condemn it, for she came from the ends of the earth to hear the wisdom of Solomon; and indeed a greater than Solomon is here"* (Matt. 12:41-42, emphasis added).

Previous generations had rejected the servants of the LORD, but that one generation alone rejected the Son of God.

Their own words will condemn them.[149] This is the teaching of the parable of the vinedressers. Having beaten, abused and sometimes killed the servants of the LORD of the vineyard, their response when the Son and Heir presented the claims of their LORD, was: *"This is the heir, come let us kill him"* (Matt. 21:38). The judgement will be inclusive, that is, all the martyrs of the *T'nach* who were rejected as messengers of God, will also rise up against this generation because He was the One to whom all prophecy was pointing, for He was the greatest prophet of all: *"the Word became flesh"* (John 1:14). Matthew reports the words of Jesus directly: *"Therefore you are witnesses against yourselves that you are sons of those who murdered the prophets. Fill up, then, the measure of your fathers' guilt. Serpents, brood of vipers!* **How can you escape the condemnation of hell?** *Therefore, indeed, I send you prophets, wise men, and scribes: some of them you will kill and crucify, and some of them you will scourge in your synagogues and persecute from city to city, that on you may come all the righteous blood shed on the earth, from the blood of righteous Abel to the blood of Zechariah, son of Berechiah, whom you murdered between the temple and the altar. Assuredly, I say to you, all these things will come upon* **this generation**" (Matt. 23:31-36).

Because of the rejection of the Messiah, the offer of the New Covenant to the nation was deferred. It will require the national leaders of Israel to call on Jesus in repentance and supplication and accept Him as Messiah and LORD. There is no guarantee that they will ever do this of their own accord, but prophecy alerts us to the time when the nation will suffer great persecution. They will be brought to the end of their resources. At that time, the LORD will pour out upon them the spirit of grace and supplication and they will repent in the words of Isaiah 53, *"He was wounded for our transgressions, He was bruised for our iniquities; The chastisement for our peace was upon Him, And by His stripes we are healed. All we like sheep have gone astray; We have turned, every one, to his own way; And the LORD has laid on Him the iniquity of us all"* (Isa. 53:5-6). Then the Messiah will return with power and great glory to save them, and the New Covenant will come into

---

149   Matt. 23:31-36

its full glory. But in the meantime, as Peter indicated on the day of Pentecost, individual Israelites did not need to wait for that future day. The blessings of the New Covenant were available immediately to them if they would reject the decision of their leaders, turn to Jesus in repentance and supplication, and take Him as Messiah and LORD. In the mercy of God these Israelites who had been involved in those events that led to the judgment of God were re-offered the opportunity to recognize Jesus as Messiah. Peter encouraged them to re-examine the evidence and escape the blanket judgment upon the nation. The preaching of the early Church leaders made the same points, that the crucified Messiah had been raised and exalted, and salvation was available for those who received Him as such, that is, as LORD and Messiah. But what about Gentiles, that is those who had not previously been Jewish proselytes? To this subject we now turn.

The New Covenant as it applies to the Gentiles

There is no ambiguity about the declaration of Jeremiah in respect of the New Covenant. It is for the Hebrew people, those of the houses of Judah and Israel. Yet the same offer of salvation under that Covenant was made to both Jew and Gentile by those commissioned to be the spokesmen of the Messiah. Did they take too much upon themselves? Did they widen the offer without authorization? Many thought so. There were large numbers in the early Church that supported those who taught that a Gentile should become a Jewish proselyte before being allowed the benefits of a Covenant relationship with God. They were mainly converted Pharisees. They believed the only door that was open was labeled 'Jews only'. Therefore circumcision and obedience to the Law of Moses were pre-requisites for entrance into the new community. Even Peter, true Jew that he was, had difficulty in considering even the possibility of the Gentiles being admitted without first converting to Judaism. It took the personal intervention of the risen Messiah to change his mind-set.

Luke, in his history of the events of that period lays out three conversions that indicate the movement of the gospel from being only Jewish or Jewish/Gentile to being available to non-Jews. The first seven chapters deal with events in Jerusalem after the ascension of Jesus. It details the birth of the Christian Church, with thousands converted, all of them Jewish, and Peter at the heart of it all. Then the history turns to those conversions that demonstrate the widening of the offer of the gospel. In chapters 8, 9, and 10 of the Acts of the Apostles, Luke, the consummate historian, records how the gospel changed the lives of three individuals, an African statesman, a Jewish Rabbi and a Roman centurion.

The African Statesman. Here is a man, evidently a person who had embraced the religion of the Jews, returning to Ethiopia where he held high office in government. He was in his chariot reading from the scroll of Isaiah the prophet—that is, a portion of the sacred writings of the Jews. He had been up to Jerusalem to attend a festival, and bought the scroll while he was there. Philip, himself a new Christian, met with him and asked if he understood what he was reading. He was reading that part of the Isaiah prophecy that said, *'In His humiliation He was deprived of justice. Who can speak of His descendants? For His life was taken from the earth"* (Acts 8:33-34). The Ethiopian asked Philip, *"… of whom does the prophet say this, of himself or of some other man?"* (Acts 8:34). Philip explained Isaiah was speaking of the Messiah who was to come and die for the sins of the Jews. The Ethiopian, already educated regarding the Jewish Messiah - it had been the main subject of conversation and speculation while he had been in Jerusalem - was able to understand the principle of the substitutionary nature of the death of Jesus of Nazareth, the Son of God and Redeemer of Israel. He asked if he could become a Christian, and be baptized. Philip said, *"If you believe with all your heart, you may"* (Acts 8:37). The African responded, not only in the affirmative, but with the formula that was declared to be the foundational doctrine of the new community, the Church of the Messiah. He said, *"I believe that Jesus Christ (Messiah) is the Son of God"* (Acts 8:37). He was baptized there and then.

The Jewish Rabbi. Saul of Tarsus, Rabbi and special envoy of the Jewish leaders in Jerusalem, was given letters of authority to extradite and imprison any followers of Jesus who had fled to Damascus. He himself was to execute the extradition warrant. He was on this mission, and had almost reached Damascus when he had a traumatic experience. He was blinded by the glory of God, and heard a voice speaking to him out of heaven. It was Jesus Himself, asking *"Saul, Saul, why are you persecuting me?"* (Acts 9:4). He fell to the ground and acknowledged that Jesus was alive and the true Messiah of Israel: *"So he, trembling and astonished, said, 'LORD, what do You want me to do?' Then the LORD said to him, 'Arise and go into the city, and you will be told what you must do'"* (Acts 9:6). What did the ascended and glorified Messiah commission Paul to do? Ananias, a disciple of Jesus, living in Damascus, was given the first intimation of the high profile mission that Paul was to undertake: *"He is a chosen vessel of Mine to bear My name **before Gentiles**, kings, and the children of Israel"* (Acts 9:15). Note here that it is the risen Messiah that authorizes the widening of the New Covenant to embrace not only the children of Israel, but also Gentiles. The offer of the gospel to non-Jewish nations was not an initiative thought up by the early Church leaders – it was an initiative imposed from the throne of God.

This should not have been a surprise to those who were students of the *T'nach*. Isaiah had already indicated that the suffering servant of Jehovah should not only be the Saviour of Israel but also a light to the Gentiles. *"**It is too small a thing** that You should be My Servant To raise up the tribes of Jacob, And to restore the preserved ones of Israel; I will also give You **as a light to the Gentiles**, That You should be My salvation **to the ends of the earth**"* (Isa. 49:6). This was a great support and strength to the Saviour, especially in the garden of Gethsemane when He faced His final rejection with its associated death sentence. To limit the benefit of the sacrifice of the Son of God to just the Hebrew race is, in the words of Scripture, *"too small a thing"*. His sacrifice and the salvation it purchased must be available to all peoples, that is, *"to the ends of the earth"*. Matthew, when he wrote his gospel, understood that the Gentiles were included and wrote of another prophetic utterance from Isaiah. The curious quote was inserted in the narrative of the twelfth chapter of his biography when the official rejection of the Messianic claim of Jesus was about to be confirmed. The Isaiah prophecy was, *"Behold! My Servant whom I have chosen, My Beloved in whom My soul is well pleased! I will put My Spirit upon Him, And **He will declare justice to the Gentiles.** He will not quarrel nor cry out, Nor will anyone hear His voice in the streets. A bruised reed He will not break, And smoking flax He will not quench, Till He sends forth justice to victory; **And in His name Gentiles will trust**"* (Matt. 12:17-21). Matthew, writing for a Jewish readership, is indicating that if Israel would not receive Jesus as Messiah, many of the Gentiles would. Luke's writing also made the point. When he gave the history of the birth of Jesus, he recorded the event that took place in the Temple when the infant Messiah was presented to the LORD. An elderly Israelite Simeon took up the baby into his arms and said to the LORD, *"...my eyes have seen Your salvation which You have prepared before the face of all peoples, **A light to bring revelation to the Gentiles**, And the glory of Your people Israel"* (Luke 2:30-32).

The Roman Centurion. The third conversion is that of Cornelius, a soldier in the employ of Rome, who was a 'God-fearer'. He already had some knowledge of the Jewish religion, and demonstrated his generous disposition by acts of kindness and gifts of money to the local synagogue. Peter was instructed to visit him and preach the gospel. To overcome Peter's reluctance to visit a non-Jew, the Messiah sent instructions from heaven. Peter had a vision of a sheet let down from heaven with many different animals in it. He was instructed to "kill and eat". But he was an observant Jew and, as he thought, under Mosaic Law. He had been taught to discern between clean and unclean, and some of these animals were designated unclean. Peter objected to the divine command. He said, *"Not so, LORD! For I have never eaten anything common or unclean"* (Acts 10:14). Three times he received the command before the vision ended. So when Peter was asked to go to the home of Cornelius, Peter, who would normally have refused, accepted the invitation. When he arrived there, he first explained how the Lord had overcome his reluctance. Then he spoke of the person and work of Jesus, the Messiah. But before Peter came to the end of his message the Spirit of God had fallen on the assembled company, a clear witness that they had been accepted for salvation. This Gentile household was the first among the non-Jewish population to embrace Christianity. To seal their conversions they were baptized.

In summarizing these three important personal experiences, there are some things to remark on. Placed as they are in Luke's history, it suggests that they are representative of certain groups of people. These three conversions contain valuable indicators that show how the New Covenant gravitated from a national, fully Jewish environment to an international Jewish/ Gentile environment.

This group is made up of representatives from the three main people groups recognized by the Hebrew nation; **a Jewish proselyte** (the Ethiopian statesman), a **Hebrew of Hebrews** (Rabbi Shaul), and **a Gentile** (the Roman Centurion).

They also represent the three main population streams that rose from the sons of Noah, that is, Ham, Shem and Japheth. The Ethiopian is from **Africa (Ham);** the Centurion is from **Europe (Japheth)** and Saul is a **Jew (Shem).** They are evidence of the truth expressed by Paul, the gospel of the Messiah *"is the power of God to salvation for everyone who believes, for the Jew first and also for the Greek* (Gentile*)"* (Rom. 1:16). So that in Jesus *"there is neither Jew nor Greek, there is neither slave nor free, there is neither male nor female"* (Gal. 3:28) for all are one in Him.

In addition, there are elements of the gospel highlighted which indicate the means by which the gospel is effected. With the African the **Word of God** is central, he was reading from Isaiah, giving Philip the opportunity to explain that Jesus was the Messiah predicted in the *T'nach*. Clearly, this feature is central to all conversions because *"faith comes by hearing, and hearing by the word of God"* (Rom. 10:17). However, in Luke's history, Saul's experience revolved around **the Lord** – it was a personal encounter with the risen Messiah. Here is emphasized the centrality of the person of Jesus in salvation. Paul himself will give the only answer possible when asked *"what must I do* *to be saved?"* (Acts 16:30). *"Believe on the Lord Jesus Christ, and you will be saved"* (Acts 16:31). With Cornelius the descent of **the Spirit of God** upon the household is the dominant feature. Again, without the work of the Spirit of God there can be no salvation: *"no one can say that Jesus is Lord except by the Holy Spirit"* (1 Cor. 12:3).

And could we not say that the whole salvific act of Jesus, the death, resurrection and ascension, is incorporated here. **His death** is evident in the Isaiah passage that the Ethiopian read, and no doubt, central in the witness of Philip. The **resurrection** is key in the experience that Paul had on the Damascus road. That Jesus had been resurrected and was alive was the truth that Paul had to grapple with. And while not specifically identified in the narrative, it was the **ascended** Christ that poured out the Spirit upon the Centurion's household in a similar fashion to that which took place on the day of Pentecost.[150]

A last comment on these significant personal encounters – the personnel involved were Peter, the individual who had authority from the Messiah to open the door of salvation to Jew and Gentile, and who later became the apostle to the Jews; Philip the evangelist, a man gifted of the Holy Spirit, who was himself a gift to the Church;[151] and of course the one person who will dominate the second half of the book of Acts and begin to take the gospel to the ends of the earth – Saul, later known as Paul, the apostle to the Gentiles. This particular conversion was of such importance that the Saviour took personal control of the event, and Saul's meeting with the resurrected Christ became a cornerstone of his defense of his apostolic commission.[152] Let us tabulate these truths and see them all side by side.

---

150   Acts 2:33
151   Eph. 4:11
152   1 Cor. 9:1

Acts 8:26 ff	Acts 9:1 ff	Acts 10:1 ff
Personal Details	**Personal Details**	**Personal Details**
Ethiopian Statesman	Jewish Rabbi	Roman Centurion
Jewish Proselyte	Jew (Hebrew	Gentile
Descendent of Ham	of Hebrews)	Descendent of
	Descendent of Shem	Japheth
Emphasis:	**Emphasis:**	**Emphasis:**
Word of God &	Person of Jesus &	Spirit of God &
Christ Crucified	Christ Resurrected	Christ Ascended
Result:	**Result:**	**Result:**
Saved and Baptized	Saved and Baptized	Saved and Baptized

It is the Death of the Messiah that makes the blessings of the New Covenant available to the Gentiles

From the foregoing it can be suggested that the inclusion of the Gentiles in the New Covenant was not something initiated by the followers of Jesus, but rather the work of the Spirit of God fulfilling the will of God. But on what grounds could a righteous God include a group of people into a Covenant which did not initially name them? Let us return to the first and foundational covenant, the Abrahamic Covenant. The Abrahamic Covenant had three main facets–dealing with the 'Seed,' the 'Land' and the 'Blessing'. The 'Seed' aspect dealt with the posterity of Abraham, and in particular included a particular member of his descendents who would be Messiah and King. The Davidic Covenant was the offspring of the 'seed' aspect in the Abrahamic Covenant which designated that the future ruler and Saviour of the nation would come from the line of David. The 'land' aspect dealt with the homeland prepared for the 'seed' of Abraham, it would be the place where the 'seed' would be planted. The Land Covenant was the offspring of the 'land' feature in the Abrahamic Covenant and was used among other things to motivate the people to remain faithful to the God of Abraham. But the main feature, indeed the predominant feature was the 'Blessing' aspect, which declared that Abraham was to be blessed, the posterity of Abraham was to be blessed, and those that blessed Abraham or his posterity were to be blessed, indeed all families of the earth could be blessed in Abraham. The clauses that speak of blessing are inclusive not exclusive, and therefore must include Gentiles in the blessing of Abraham. Now the New Covenant is the offspring of the 'blessing' aspect of the Abrahamic Covenant, and if it is to be true to the intention of the Abrahamic Covenant, must likewise be inclusive and not exclusive, that is, must include all nations and families. Therefore, to understand the New Covenant as being available to all people is not to insert something foreign into its structure, but rather is interpreting the covenant in the light of its parent Covenant that was declared in the first book of the *T'nach*.

It can be assumed that Peter and the other apostles that travelled with Jesus received instructions to make the New Covenant immediately available when they were taught by the risen Messiah during the period between the resurrection morning and the ascension. However, the inclusion of the Gentiles, while imposed on Peter as the keeper of the keys, seemed to wait for Saul to develop the doctrine. Saul, a man also taught directly by the Messiah, understood very early that the inclusion of the Gentiles in the New Covenant could be traced back to the Abrahamic Covenant.

We have already considered how he described the Mosaic Covenant as a wall of separation between Jew and Gentile. That during the period of the Law it precluded the Gentiles from any access to the covenant blessings of Israel. He wrote: *"at that time you were without Christ, being **aliens from the commonwealth of Israel and strangers from the covenants of promise,** having no hope and without God in the world"* (Eph. 2:12, emphasis added). The Gentiles were first excluded by the Law of Moses, a wall of partition. But the death of the Messiah was the 'end' of the Law,[153] that is, the purpose and goal of the Law had been accomplished. 'End' (Gk. *telos*) here is usually considered to mean "termination, the limit at which a thing ceases to be (always of the end

---

153   Rom. 10:4

of some act or state, but not of the end of a period of time)," or "the end to which all things relate, the aim, purpose."[154] Here, it is suggested, it carries both meanings. It was terminated because it had achieved its goal. It was no longer needed. So the middle wall of partition became unnecessary. Paul speaks of it being broken down. *"For He ... has broken down the middle wall of separation"* (Eph. 2:14) which means Gentiles now have access to the covenant blessings of Israel. *"Now, therefore, you are no longer strangers and foreigners, but fellow citizens with the saints and members of the household of God"* (Eph. 2:19).

The extent of the inclusion is spelt out for us. *"For He Himself is our peace, who has made both one, and has broken down the middle wall of separation, having abolished in His flesh the enmity, that is, the law of commandments contained in ordinances, so as to create in Himself one new man from the two, thus making peace, and that He might reconcile them both to God in one body through the cross, thereby putting to death the enmity. And He came and preached peace to you who were afar off and to those who were near. For through Him we both have access by one Spirit to the Father"* (Eph. 2:14-18). This means there is now no difference between the Jew and the Gentile in respect of the blessing of salvation that the New Covenant provides. Peter, the keeper of the keys, said it first, *"So God, who knows the heart, acknowledged them by giving them the Holy Spirit, just as He did to us, and made* **no distinction between us and them***, purifying their hearts by faith"* (Acts 15:8-9). And Paul confirmed it when he dealt with the place of Israel in the purposes of God (Romans chapters nine through eleven). He said, **"there is no distinction between Jew and Greek**, *for the same* LORD *over all is rich to all who call upon Him"* (Rom. 10:12). In other words, the Church comes into blessing under the Abrahamic Covenant, because Christ, in His death, did away with the Law of Moses, the wall that separated Jew and Gentile. Paul, a Hebrew of Hebrews, wrote: *"Christ has redeemed us from the curse of the law, having become a curse for us (for it is written, 'Cursed is everyone who hangs on a tree'), that* **the blessing of Abraham might come upon the Gentiles in Christ Jesus***, that we might receive the*

---

154   Strongs Greek Dictionary #5056

promise of the Spirit through faith" (Gal. 3:13-14, emphasis added). This indicates that we can share in the blessing of Abraham. His argument, of course, is that this can only be so if the Gentile has similar faith to Abraham, and the evidence of that faith, in the context of the current dispensation, is faith in the Messiah of Israel, Jesus. *"Just as Abraham 'believed God, and it was accounted to him for righteousness.' Therefore know that only those who are of faith are sons of Abraham"* (Gal. 3:6-7). This maintains then that we are children of Abraham by faith, and therefore have access to the New Covenant. This, of course, raises further questions which should be considered. First, if the middle wall of partition has been broken down and the Gentiles have access by faith to the Abrahamic Covenant, what does this mean for Gentile participation in the 'seed' aspect and the 'land' aspect? These questions, while important, are almost supplementary to the main question that has troubled the Church for centuries. Does this doctrine mean that the Church has replaced Israel in the purposes of God? It is to these questions we must now turn.

Chapter 20
The Church and the Abrahamic Covenant

The Church and the 'Seed' Aspect of the Abrahamic Covenant

It is clear from Scripture that part of the covenant purpose for the 'seed' or posterity of Abraham was:

1. to produce a nation that could be segregated, educated and trained to worship and serve the one and only God. They were to be the trail-blazers of monotheism.

2. to understand the principles of righteousness.

3. to be a 'sign' nation for all other nations in respect of monotheism and righteousness.

4. to receive and protect the future Saviour of the human race.

How successful were they? Answer: very successful:

1. they embraced segregation wholeheartedly, and committed themselves to following the principles and precepts laid down for them by the God they worshiped and served.

2. their offerings and festivals demonstrated what was required to be accepted before a righteous God. Moreover, their writings gave such principles a voice, which could be heard by those who would take time to listen.

3. that they became a 'sign' nation has also been evident. They have survived against all odds, and those that have cursed them have themselves been cursed.

4. and whatever else you say about the generations that

were contemporary with the Messiah, Israel did provide an environment where He, a sinless law abiding individual, could grow up and follow the code of righteousness without being the object of foolish curiosity and scrutiny. Apart from the opposition of Herod the Great at His birth, He spent the first thirty years in relative anonymity, just as was intended.

Furthermore, it was intended that after the nation had received their Messiah and the Messianic kingdom was a reality, they would continue with the essentials expressed above. The New Covenant would be in place, and they would be the evidence to the world that the LORD was a covenant keeping God, and that under His reign, government would be righteous and equitable; all people would be treated equally, and none would be disadvantaged. Unfortunately, for the people of Israel, the decision taken by their national leaders has delayed for them the implementation of the Messianic kingdom and the New Covenant. Nevertheless, God's purposes continue to be fulfilled. The Abrahamic Covenant being an eternal covenant is still in place, which means that the nation of Israel still holds the privileged position of being the 'seed' to which the foundational covenant applies.

But since 'seed' singular is also taken by Paul to refer to the Messiah, and He has already come, then for the nation of Israel as well as the Church, the main element of the 'seed' aspect has been fulfilled. And even though the Church comes into blessing under the Abrahamic Covenant, at no time do its Gentile members become Jews and the 'seed' of Abraham in the natural sense.

Let us compare and contrast Israel and the Church

This comparison is needed because Abraham is the father of the Hebrew race, and also considered to be Father of the faithful.[155] First the differences:

1. Israel's future blessings are situated on earth, whereas the Church's future blessings are situated in heaven. In His wisdom God provides a place for Israel on earth. Designated under the Abrahamic Covenant, they will fully occupy the Promised Land during the millennial reign of the Messiah, and even when there is a new heaven and a new earth; Israel's distant future will still be on earth, that is, the new earth that John saw

    In contrast, God provides a heavenly future for the Church. It is true that there will be duties on earth for the Church during the millennial reign of Christ but her citizenship is in heaven, and that will be her home when the heavens are recreated. The first difference then is this: Israel's future is tied to earth, whereas the Church's future is tied to heaven.

2. While Abraham is set forward in Scripture as Father to Israel and also Father of the faithful, it is significant that his seed is described under two figures. The dust of the earth (Gen. 13:16), and the stars of heaven (Gen. 15:5) surely reflecting that every provision for the nation of Israel is terrestrial, even to the degree of inheriting a homeland on the renewed earth; whereas the provisions for the Church are mainly celestial.

    The two posterities of the Abrahamic covenant are given by Paul, "Therefore it is of faith that it might be according to grace, so that the promise might be sure to all the seed, not only to those who are of the law, but also to those who are of the faith of Abraham, who is the father of us all" (Rom. 4:16).

3. Israelites become what they are by physical birth. They are members of the Hebrew race if their parents

---

155   These comparisons are based on those included in Lewis Sperry Chafer's Systematic Theology (1993). Originally published: Dallas, Tex. : Dallas Seminary Press, 1947-1948. (4:47). Grand Rapids, MI: Kregel Publications.

were Hebrews, or at least one parent. It is automatic. Paul suggested he could have boasted of his lineage for he was a 'Hebrew of Hebrews', that is, both his mother and father were Hebrews. There is even a suggestion that all four grandparents were also Hebrews. The point is that it is natural generation; they are each one begotten of human parents.

Christians become what they are by spiritual birth. They are 'born of God' and are therefore His legitimate offspring. A Jew is a child of Abraham, but a Christian (whether Jew or Gentile) is a child of God.

4. This means that Abraham is the head of the Jewish race. They are Abraham's children whereas Christ is the head of the Church. They are God's children.

5. God has made several covenants with the nation of Israel, and He will yet make another covenant, the New Covenant, with them,[156] which will replace the Mosaic Covenant. However, the benefits of the New Covenant are currently enjoyed by the Church. The blessings of the New Covenant are future for Israel, but present for the Church.

6. Israel is a nation, and fits in among the nations of the world. The Church is not a nation, indeed is made up of people from all nations,[157] including Israel, and has no citizenship here, "for our citizenship is in heaven" (Phil. 3:20). The members of the Church are considered pilgrims and strangers on the earth.

7. In the purposes of God, Israel was appointed to be a witness to the one and only true God. They were to demonstrate that "righteousness exalts a nation, But sin is a reproach to any people", (Prov. 14:34) and by it exercise an influence over the nations of the earth. They should have been a light to the Gentiles, long

---

156   The timing of the Covenant is suggested by Rom. 11:26-27

157   Rev. 5:9

before the Messiah was born.

The Psalmist captured this aspect exactly (Ps. 67:1-7)."*God be merciful to us and bless us, And cause His face to shine upon us, Selah* **That Your way may be known on earth, Your salvation among all nations.** *Let the peoples praise You, O God; Let all the peoples praise You. Oh, let the nations be glad and sing for joy! For You shall judge the people righteously, And govern the nations on earth. Selah Let the peoples praise You, O God; Let all the peoples praise You. Then the earth shall yield her increase; God, our own God, shall bless us. God shall bless us, And all the ends of the earth shall fear Him*" (Ps. 67:1-7).

This will be accomplished in a coming age; nevertheless historically there was very little missionary undertaking. The rules of separation were so enforced that generally Gentiles were disparaged as the 'uncircumcised'. Mostly Israel faced inward toward the tabernacle or temple and nearly all her prayers were of the 'bless me and mine' category.

In contra-distinction to this, immediately upon her formation, the Church was constituted a foreign missionary society. It is true that it took some divine intervention to give it momentum; nevertheless, we are indebted to the early Church for the Biblical pattern of missionary evangelism, a pattern that has been taken up many times. The Church recognizes her obligation to evangelize the people of the earth in each generation.

8. To Israel God is known by His primary titles, but not as the Father of the individual Israelite. In distinction to this, the Christian is actually begotten of God and has every right to address Him as Father.

9. To Israel, Christ is Messiah, Immanuel, and King with all that those titles imply. To the Church, Christ is Saviour, LORD, Bridegroom, and Head. Jesus is King of Israel but LORD of the Church. He is not King of the Church.

10. Under the dispensation of the Law, the Spirit of God came upon an individual Israelite on rare occasions. The bulk of the population knew nothing of the anointing of the Spirit. Those selected for special service received special equipping but all others were strangers to a personal anointing. Moreover, the Spirit would withdraw as soon as the service was completed. In contrast the Christian is not only begotten of the Spirit[158] but indwelt by the Spirit; in truth, it is the main evidence of his/her salvation.[159]

11. For one and a half millennia the Law of Moses was Israel's rule of daily life. It is written: "But the mercy of the LORD is from everlasting to everlasting On those who fear Him, And His righteousness to children's children, To such as keep His covenant, And to those who remember His commandments to do them" (Ps. 103:17-18).

    Unlike this, the members of Christ's Body, are "not under law but under grace" (Rom. 6:14). This does not mean there is nothing expected of the Christian – but it is phrased more like a request than a command. For example, Romans 12:1: *"I beseech you therefore, brethren, by the mercies of God, that you present your bodies a living sacrifice, holy, acceptable to God, which is your reasonable service."*

12. The weakness of the dispensation of Law was that it provided no assistance to the child of Abraham to fulfill its commands. Consequently, its failure was inevitable because of weakness of the flesh.[160] The children of God, in contrast, receive additional resources to meet every expectation placed on them. The indwelling Spirit of God has access to the riches of grace, and makes them available to the believer who wishes to

---

158   John 3:1-8
159   Rom. 8:9
160   Rom. 8:3

draw on them.[161]

13. After His final visit to the Temple, Jesus spoke of the future that Israel would suffer in light of His rejection. It would be one of exile and persecution, culminating in a period of tribulation which would only end when the nation's leaders would recognize His Messianic claim and call for Him to rescue them.[162]

On the other hand, in a totally different vein, the night before His execution, He spoke to the disciples of the future for his followers. In their life they might face difficulties, but they would have the aid of the 'Comforter' who would strengthen them, guide them, and teach them. Furthermore, for every one who died they would be received into the immediate presence of the Messiah. The future for them was the same whether they lived or died, they would know the immediate presence of God.

When these two discourses are put side by side they demonstrate the wide differences that exist between Israel and the Church.

14. As seen in His words specifically addressed to Israel, Christ returns to her as her King in power and great glory,[163] at which time she will be gathered from every part of the earth by angelic ministration and into her own land.[164]

Over against these great events promised to Israel is the return of Christ for His own Bride, when He takes her with Him into heaven's glory,[165] where the marriage will take place.[166]

15. Isaiah declared, "But thou, Israel, art My servant"

161 Phil. 4:19
162 The Olivet discourse – Matt.23.37-25.46
163 Matt.24.30; Mark 13.26; Luke 21.27
164 Deut. 30:1–8; Jer. 23:7–8; Matt. 24:31
165 2 Cor.11.2; John 14.1-3
166 Rev. 19:6-8

(Isa. 41:8, KJV). Though individuals in Israel attained to great usefulness, as did the prophets, priests, and kings, yet they never reached a higher distinction than that they were the servants of Jehovah.

Contrariwise, the individuals who compose the Church, while they do serve, are not classed as servants, but are members of the family of God, are 'in Christ' and betrothed to Him.

16. When Jesus returns and sets up His throne in Jerusalem He will reign over Israel as absolute sovereign and the Jewish people will be His subjects. In this task he will be assisted (not that He needs assistance!) by David[167] and the apostles that accompanied Him at the time of His first coming.[168] Those of the elect nation are appointed to be subjects in His earthly kingdom.

The reign of the Messiah from His throne in Jerusalem will also extend to all nations and it will be the Church (the Bride of Christ) who will co-reign with Him over the Gentile nations.[169]

17. The arrangements in Israel included the separation of the descendents of Aaron to form the Aaronic priesthood. They were responsible for intercession for both the nation and individual Israelites. No one else was allowed to usurp the sacerdotal duties that rightfully belonged to the priesthood.

The Church on the other hand is totally populated by those who are priests, that is, they do not need an intermediary but are able to enter the presence of God directly.[170]

18. The Aaronic High Priest of Israel could only have access into the immediate presence of God once a year

---

167   Ezek. 37:21-28
168   Matt. 19:28
169   Rev. 20:4-6
170   John 16.23

and that with limitations.[171] The Melchizedekian High Priest of the Church, Jesus, is in the presence of the Father continually as her advocate, intercessor and representative.

19. At no time could the High Priest invite another Israelite to enter the Holy of Holies in Temple or Tabernacle, but Jesus because His sacrifice was accepted 'once and for all', through the inspired writer, offers that invitation. *"Seeing then that we have a great High Priest who has passed through the heavens, Jesus the Son of God, let us hold fast our confession (and) let us therefore come boldly to the throne of grace, that we may obtain mercy and find grace to help in time of need"* (Heb. 4:14-16).

20. As a nation, Israel is likened by Jehovah to His wife—a wife untrue and yet to be restored.[172] In marked distinction to this situation respecting Israel, is the revelation that the Church is to Christ as an espoused virgin to be married in heaven.[173]

From the foregoing, it is evident that there are significant differences between the natural 'seed' of Abraham, the ethnic group that is Israel; and the 'seed' of Abraham, the Church, constituted so by faith.

But while there are contrasts between Israel and the Church, it should be observed that, in certain respects, there are similarities between these two groups of people, which are only to be expected. It is still the same God, with the same principles of righteousness. He will always act in love and mercy and will always be found of the individual who would seek Him with all their heart.

1. Both Israel and the Church have a relationship to God

---

171 See chapter 15 and 16 in The Messiah and the Feasts of Israel by the same author.

172 Jer. 3:1, 14, 20; 31.31-34; Ezek. 16:1–59; Hos. 2:1–23; Isa. 54:1–17; cf. Gal. 4:27

173 2 Cor. 11:2; Rev. 19:7–9

which at rock bottom stands on the ground of faith. Salvation through all dispensations will be 'by grace alone, through faith alone, in God alone'. The only difference is the means by which God's mercy is dispensed.

2. So each, in turn, has its own peculiar relation to God, to righteousness, to sin, to redemption, to salvation, to human responsibility, and to destiny.

3. They are each witnesses to the Word of God; each may claim the same Shepherd; they have doctrines in common; the death of Christ avails in its own way for each; they are alike loved with an everlasting love; and each, as determined by God, will be glorified.

The similarities, in part, have given rise to a doctrine of replacement, that is, that since the language of Scripture speaks of the Church in a similar way to that which treats of Israel, then the Church, the entity brought into being subsequent to the rejection of Jesus as Israel's Messiah, must be Israel's replacement. It is suggested that the Church is now the true 'seed' of Abraham; that the circumcision of the heart is the true 'circumcision'. Those that hold to this view of Scripture believe that the Church has superseded Israel in the purposes of God. This doctrine has been held by the majority of believers since the second century A.D. But is it correct? No doubt, the reader already understands that this writer does not subscribe to replacement theology. But on what grounds? We will examine the replacement view in the next chapter, but before that we can take a look at the land aspect of the Abrahamic Covenant.

The Church and the 'land' aspect of the Abrahamic Covenant

The treatment of this subject will, of necessity, be very brief. In the Abrahamic Covenant the land was promised to the natural 'seed' of Abraham as a homeland. The Abrahamic Covenant is an eternal, unconditional covenant. Therefore, the Jewish people will receive it, and occupy it as promised. The Land will live up to its description of fruitfulness, that is, a land flowing with milk and honey.[174] It will be a place of peace and safety and righteousness will be its hallmark. Its inhabitants will work and be productive and enjoy not only the fruits of their labour but also all aspects of life under the watchful eye of the God that neither slumbers nor sleeps.[175] Jerusalem will be the capital city of the world, and the throne of David will be set up there, in fulfillment of the Davidic Covenant. It will be from Jerusalem that Jesus will reign when He returns. In view of the foregoing, it can be stated clearly – the Church has no title to the land of Israel, nor in the will of God, will she occupy it at any time. It has been promised to the ethnic race of Israel and they will inherit and inhabit it. It will require the nation to return to the God of Jacob and receive Jesus as Messiah, Son of David and Son of God – this they will do – as foretold by the prophets of Israel.

---

174   Isa. 30:23-26; 35:1-2; 65:21-24; etc.
175   Ps. 121:4; Jer. 31:1-6; 11-14; Ezek. 34:25-31. etc

Chapter 21
Has the Church Replaced Israel in the Purposes of God?

It is necessary to consider this subject because we maintain that the Church came into blessing on the grounds of a covenant which the LORD made with Israel – a covenant, which according to Scripture, has not yet been implemented for them as a nation. The replacement view maintains that the dynamics of the implementation of the New Covenant has removed Israel as the beneficiary of the Covenant and substituted them with the Church. They maintain that this major shift in divine policy was made as a result of Israel's national rejection of Jesus, their Messiah. Stated simply - because they rejected their Messiah, God rejected them, and replaced them with the Church. Consequently the Church inherited the covenant blessings originally promised to Israel. Thomas Ice said that replacement theology "is the view that the Church has permanently replaced Israel through which God works and that national Israel does not have a future in the plan of God."[176] Replacement theologian, Bruce K. Waltke said, "The hard fact (is) that national Israel and its law have been permanently replaced by the Church and the New Covenant."[177] We need to be very sure of our ground here, because we began by stating that a main feature of God's

---

176   Thomas Ice, <u>What do you do with a future National Israel in the Bible</u>, The Thomas Ice Collection, n.d., p. 2.

177   Bruce K. Waltke, <u>Kingdom Promises as Spiritual</u>, in Continuity and Discontinuity, 274 (quoted by Michael J. Vlach in his dissertation 'The Church as a Replacement of Israel" p.12)

glory was His *Hesed ve-hemet.*[178] *hesed* is His loving kindness, that quality that involves acts of beneficence, mutuality, and those obligations that flow from a legal relationship. *hemet,* usually translated "truth," encompasses reliability, durability, and faithfulness. The combination of the two terms expresses God's absolute and eternal dependability in dispensing His benefactions. If He has, even in the smallest degree, withdrawn any element of an unconditional covenant with His ancient people, then the concept of the glory of God being best seen in His faithfulness and reliability must be undermined.

It is true that the national implementation of the New Covenant for Israel was delayed because of the national rejection of the Messianic claim of Jesus, but as we have already indicated, the New Covenant was activated by the Messiah for individual Israelites if they qualified to benefit from it. In other words, individual Jews who accepted Jesus as Messiah became beneficiaries under the New Covenant. Let us restate our view that while the national implementation of the Covenant is yet future, the execution of the Covenant for individual Jews is current.[179] Every Israelite who acknowledges the person and work of *Yeshua HaMashiac* (Jesus the Messiah) comes under the New Covenant and is 'born again' (to use a Jewish term). We also believe that Gentiles can come into blessing on the same grounds, that is, on the basis of the New Covenant, by acknowledging the person and work of Jesus the Messiah, Son of David, Son of God.[180] This comes about because of the desire of the LORD that His salvation should reach the ends of the earth.[181]

That the door was opened to the Gentiles to 'share' in the blessings of the New Covenant does not mean that the multinational group of believers, corporately called 'the Church' has replaced the national ethnic group called 'Israel' in the purposes of God. But the rejection of the replacement view needs to be supported by more than statements.

---

178   Chapter 1
179   P. 84 ff
180   P. 86 ff
181   Isa. 4:6

Why should we reject the replacement view?

We should reject the replacement view because at best it implies God is duplicitous, and at worst it makes Him a liar. The plain meaning of Scripture is that God has made Covenant promises to Israel and He is expected to fulfill them. The basic Abrahamic Covenant which was the foundation for the Land, Davidic and New Covenants was established in a way to preclude any doubt. *"For when God made a promise to Abraham, because He could swear by no one greater, He swore by Himself, saying, 'Surely blessing I will bless you, and multiplying I will multiply you.' And so, after He had patiently endured, He obtained the promise. For men indeed swear by the greater, and an oath for confirmation is for them an end of all dispute. Thus God, determining to show more abundantly to the heirs of promise* **the immutability of His counsel***, confirmed it by an oath, that by two immutable things, in which it is impossible for God to lie, we might have strong consolation, who have fled for refuge to lay hold of the hope set before us. This hope we have as an anchor of the soul, both sure and steadfast, and which enters the Presence behind the veil, where the forerunner has entered for us, even Jesus, having become High Priest forever according to the order of Melchizedek"* (Heb. 6:13-20). If this Scripture means anything, it means that God does not change His mind; and remember, it was written by a Jew to other Jews. Paul, the apostle to the Gentiles wrote of the chosen people, *"Concerning ... election they are beloved for the sake of the fathers.* **For the gifts and the calling of God are irrevocable"** (Rom. 11:28-29). The dictionary meaning of irrevocable is: "not able to be changed, reversed, or recovered".[182] The Bible declares, *"God is not a man, that He should lie, Nor a son of man, that He should repent. Has He said, and will He not do? Or has He spoken, and will He not make it good?"* (Num. 23:19). The temptation in the Garden of Eden began, *"Has God indeed said?"* (Gen. 3:1). We maintain He has said – He declared that the seed of Abraham will come into the full blessing of salvation, they will know God, from the least to the greatest of them, they will inherit the Land and they will enjoy the honor of being the people of God, the wife of Jehovah

---

182   Concise Oxford English Dictionary

and His special treasure. If the Jewish people cannot rely on the Covenant promises of God, then how can Gentile believers have any confidence in God's word?

But those that contend that the New Covenant is now the possession of the Church would suggest that it did not require God to change His mind. That it is simply a matter of interpretation. They would suggest that where you read Israel in the *T'nach* you could substitute Church, for the Church was in view all along. That it was always the divine intention that Israel should be put forward in Scripture as a type of the Church. If it is said that God did not mean what He said through the Old Testament writers, but rather there was a hidden meaning beneath the text, that would seem to imply again that God is less than honest. It suggests that Israel was only commissioned to produce the environment for the birth of the Messiah, the seed of the woman, and once that purpose was accomplished the nation was superseded by the Church as His people. This scenario certainly flies in the face of what Dr. David L. Cooper, late director of the Biblical Society, put forward as the 'Golden Rule of Interpretation', that is, "When the plain sense of Scripture makes common sense, seek no other sense, therefore, take every word at its primary, ordinary, usual, literal meaning unless the facts of the immediate context, studied in the light of related passages and axiomatic and fundamental truths, indicate clearly otherwise."[183] Simply put, this law states that ALL biblical passages are to be taken exactly as they read unless something in the text indicates it should be taken some other way than literally.

But the replacement theologian will respond to say – we are not imposing this doctrine on Scripture, it arises from new revelation that is available from the inspired writers of the New Testament. Progressive revelation means that we must re-read the Old Testament in the light of the more recent revelation provided by the New. LaRondelle has stated, "the New Testament is the authorized and authoritative interpreter of the Old

---

183   See Biblical Research Studies Group at www.biblicalresearch.info/page55.html

Testament."[184] On this basis, supercessionists feel comfortable in rejecting a literal interpretation of Old Testament texts, and are able to say that the literal texts relating to Israel are now finding their spiritual fulfillment in the Church.

The difficulty with this view is that the clear statements of the Old Testament have to be re-interpreted on very flimsy grounds. It suggests that with the New Testament in our hands we are able to say that God did not mean what He said then but that He meant something else. If that is the case, would He have not included a statement to that effect in the New Testament? But there is no text that says that Israel has been permanently rejected, and been replaced by the Church. This statement, of course, would be challenged by those that hold the replacement view. They contend that there are such texts. Essential to their case is Galatians 6:16: *"And as many as walk according to this rule, peace and mercy be upon them, and upon the Israel of God"*. For their position to hold, this has to be translated as the NIV translates it: *"Peace and mercy to all who follow this rule, even to the Israel of God."* They require the Greek word *'kai'* to be translated 'even' and not 'and', thus making those who walk according to the rule previously advertised, *"the Israel of God."* Yet the most common use of *'kai'* is 'and' (the continuative or copulative (joining) sense). The second most frequent use is the adjunctive sense 'also'. The sense of 'even' (the explicative sense) is very rare. Thus the NASB; NRSV; ESV; ASV; NKJV; KJV and Darby all translate it 'and'. The Greek scholar Marvin Vincent explains, "The *'kai'* 'and' may be simply connective, in which case 'the Israel of God' may be different from 'as many as,' etc., and may mean truly converted Jews. Or the *'kai'* may be explicative, in which case 'the Israel of God' will define and emphasize 'as many as', etc., and will mean the whole body of Christians, Jewish and Gentile. In other words, they who walk according to this rule form the true Israel of God. **The explicative *'kai'* is at best doubtful here, and is rather forced,** although clear instances of it may be

---

184   Hans K. LaRondelle, The Israel of God in Prophecy, (Berrien Springs, Michigan: Andrews University Press, 1983) p.9.

found in 1 Corinthians 3:5; 15:38. **It seems better to regard it as simply connective**"[185] (emphasis added). To rely on a verse that is not rock solid in its meaning is weakening to their case.

Moreover, every other reference in both Old and New Testaments that uses the word 'Israel' uses it in its ethnic sense. You would have to have compelling reasons to change its meaning in Galatians chapter 6 verse 16 and the context does not provide those compelling reasons.

Another verse that is quoted is Romans 9:6: *"For they are not all Israel who are of Israel."* By this, it is suggested that in this reference the term Israel encompasses Gentile believers as well as Jewish believers. But this section of Romans (chapters 9 through 11) is dealing with ethnic Israel, and this verse surely must be interpreted similarly. This reference, Romans 9.6, is bracketed between two expressions of ethnic Israel. In verses 3 to 5 Paul expresses his concern regarding his Jewish brothers and sisters: *"For I could wish that I myself were accursed from Christ for my brethren, **my countrymen according to the flesh, who are Israelites,** to whom pertain the adoption, the glory, the covenants, the giving of the law, the service of God, and the promises; of whom are the fathers and from whom, according to the flesh, Christ came, who is over all, the eternally blessed God. Amen."* Then the other side of verse 6 i.e. verses 7 to 9 there is another reference to ethnic Israel, that is, the children of Abraham through Sarah: *"Nor are they all children because they are the seed of Abraham; but, 'In Isaac your seed shall be called.' That is, those who are the children of the flesh, these are not the children of God; but the children of the promise are counted as the seed. For this is the word of promise: 'At this time I will come and Sarah shall have a son'"* (Rom. 9:7-9). There is no indication that Paul is introducing a different definition of Israel between these two statements.

A more satisfying explanation of the teaching contained in the text *"they are not all Israel who are of Israel"* is that the believing remnant within the nation are identified as 'Israel' within 'Israel'. That 'Israel' is made up of believing and unbelieving

---

185   Vincent, M. R.. Word studies in the New Testament, 4:180, (Bellingham, WA: Logos Research Systems, Inc., 2002)

Jews. This would certainly be the understanding of the concept of 'Jew' in Romans 2:28-29, another verse that is used to support the view that God has replaced Israel with the Church: *"For he is not a Jew who is one outwardly, nor is circumcision that which is outward in the flesh; but he is a Jew who is one inwardly; and circumcision is that of the heart, in the Spirit, not in the letter; whose praise is not from men but from God"* (Rom. 2:28-29). What this teaches is that a real Jew is one who is a faithful, believing child of Abraham, in contrast to someone who simply relies on having been born of Jewish parents. Again, it is dealing with the difference between believing and non-believing Jews, and is not introducing the concept of Gentiles being 'spiritual Jews'. Paul, in this section, is addressing that old chestnut that the Jews invariably raised, *"We are Abraham's descendants"* (John 8:33). Their doctrine is given a voice in the Mishnah where it says, "All Israelites have a share in the world to come."[186] This doctrine declares that if you are a Jew you are safe. **"All Israelites"** have a share in the world to come. It is true that the Mishnah does subsequently make some exceptions to the "all Israelites" but they are only those who were notoriously wicked, like Ahab. Paul is arguing that all Israelites will NOT have a share in the world to come. He is following the line of reasoning that had been expressed by Jesus,[187] and John the Baptist.[188] The Messiah, the Fore-runner and the Apostle to the Gentiles would all tell you, outward observance is not enough; circumcision must be, *"of the heart"* (Rom. 2:29), that is the purpose of these verses. The distinction that Paul makes here is between Jews who trust in externals and Jews who have faith. He is not widening the concept of 'Jew' to include Gentiles. William MacDonald wrote: "A real Jew is the one who is not only a descendant of Abraham but who also manifests a godly life. This passage does not teach that all believers are Jews, or that the Church is the Israel of God. Paul is talking about those who are born of Jewish parentage and is insisting that the mere fact of birth and the ordinance of circumcision are not enough. There must also be inward

---

186   Mishnah: Sanhedrin 10:1A
187   John 8:33 ff
188   Luke 3:8

reality"[189]. Supporters of replacement theology must look elsewhere for firm ground to build on.

Another text, which supercessionists[190] consider is a help to their case is 1 Peter 2:9-10, because Peter applies a cluster of terms to the Church which had previously been applied to Israel. But if the case for supercessionism has not been proved by other texts, this one on it own cannot do it. The first question that should be asked is: 'who was Peter writing to?' when he said, 'you are a chosen race ...'. He himself tells us – they are *"sojourners of the dispersion"* (Gk. *parepidemois diasporas*) (1 Pet. 1:1). Wuest says, "the word 'scattered' is from *'diasporas'* (dispersion) and is used in John 7:35 and James 1:1, in both places referring to those Jews who were living outside of Palestine. Peter uses it in the same way. The recipients of this letter were Christian Jews."[191] That Peter is writing to the Jews of the dispersion should be expected since he is the apostle to the Jews. That He is writing to Jewish Christians is borne out by internal evidence also since he alludes to the *T'nach* on 29 occasions. In respect of the text itself, 'race' and 'nation' cannot apply to the Church but can apply to Israel. The dictionary definition of 'nation' is "a large body of people united by common descent, culture, or language, inhabiting a particular state or territory."[192] Israel fits that description exactly, whereas the Church cannot. Indeed, there are several other texts that use the word 'nation' to describe Israel, but there are none that clearly use the word 'nation' to describe the Church. And even if we allow that the text refers to the Church, all that can be maintained is that there is continuity in God's dealing with humanity. That those He takes as His own people, Israel first and then the Church, are constituted in a similar fashion. Both are chosen, are priests, are

189   William MacDonald, <u>Believer's Bible Commentary,</u> Art Farstad. (Nashville, Tennessee: Thomas Nelson Publishers, 1989) p. 1685.

190   Those that hold to the doctrine of replacement theology

191   Wuest's studies in the Greek New Testament. Wm. Eerdmans Publishing Co., Grand Rapids

192   Soanes, C., & Stevenson, A. Concise Oxford English dictionary, 11th ed., (Oxford: Oxford University Press. 2004)

holy, and belong to God. Parallelism does not indicate replacement; similarity does not prove identity.

Philippians. 3:3 contains a phrase that is also used to support the replacement point of view: *"for we are the true circumcision, who worship in the Spirit of God and glory in Christ Jesus and put no confidence in the flesh."* But what Paul is doing here is countering the false teaching that circumcision was necessary for salvation. *"Beware of the dogs, beware of the evil workers, beware of the false circumcision."* (3:2) The Old Testament rite of physical circumcision was not only a sign of covenant relationship, but it was also intended to be related to spiritual circumcision of the heart.[193] (cf. Deut. 30:6). Writing to Gentiles, Paul wants them to understand that they do not need to be physically circumcised to come into a relationship with God. They come under a covenant relationship if they had no confidence in the flesh and *"worship God in the spirit, and rejoice in Christ Jesus"* (Phil. 3:3). He is not redefining the definitions of Church and Israel. He was stating that those who had exercised faith in Christ did not need to be physically circumcised as the Jewish party contended. Salvation is based on Christ's righteousness not on the 'flesh'. To rephrase it, no-one needs to become a Jew to become a Christian.

But what about those texts which speak of Christians as the 'sons of Abraham'? Does this mean they have been constituted Jews? For example, *"Therefore, be sure that it is those who are of faith who are sons of Abraham"* (Gal. 3:7; See also Gal. 3:29 and Rom. 4:11). Replacement theologians argue that Gentile association with Abraham must mean that Gentile believers are a part of a new spiritual Israel. The logic is based on the assumption that being a son of Abraham automatically makes one a Jew. But this is not so. The argument of Scripture is that Abraham was a believer before he was circumcised. That is why believers generally are Abraham's descendents and heirs according to promise.[194] Vlach argues that "replacement theologians are too restrictive in their definition of what makes one a "son" or

---

193   Deut. 30:6
194   cf. confer, compare

"seed" of Abraham. A Gentile believer can be a "son" or a "seed" of Abraham by faith without becoming a Jew."[195] It would be different if the New Testament referred to the saints as the children or 'seed' of Jacob, or to use an Old Testament phrase, 'children of Israel' but it does not. The blessing that Gentiles enjoy comes from that element of the Abrahamic Covenant that prophesies and promises that in Abraham shall all the families of the earth be blessed, or more particularly, as Paul sees it, *"the scripture, foreseeing that God would justify the heathen through faith, preached before the gospel unto Abraham, saying, In thee shall all nations be blessed"* (Gal. 3:8, KJV, emphasis added). There is no hint here that the blessing comes upon Gentiles as a result of the promise made to Abraham that he would become a great nation. This shows that Gentiles can be 'sons of Abraham' and related to the Abrahamic covenant without becoming spiritual Jews. You do not have to become a Jew to be saved, and you do not become a Jew, even a spiritual Jew, once you have been saved.

In Ephesians 2:11-19 the work of Christ is described as including a unity between Jew and Gentile. He has made *"both groups into one"* (2:14); He made *"the two into one new man"* (2:15) and He reconciled *"both in one body"* (2:16). Does this mean that the Gentiles have been incorporated into a new, redefined Israel? This text does not refer to the Gentiles being incorporated into a redefined Israel but rather Jewish believers and Gentile believers are brought together into a new entity, a new creation, *"one new man"* – the Church. That Jewish believers have been brought into the Church does not erase God's purposes for ethnic Israel.

Much of the material that fuels replacement theology comes from the fact that the nation rejected their Messiah, and accepted their part in His crucifixion when they said, *"His blood be on us and on our children"* (Matt. 27:25). It is true that Jesus, anticipating His execution warned the chief priests and elders of the nation, saying, *"Therefore I say to you, the kingdom of God will be taken from you and given to a nation bearing the fruits of it"* (Matt. 21:43). This, it is suggested, supports the view that Israel lost their place in the purposes of God, and was replaced by

---

195   Gal. 3:29 (see also Rom. 4:8-18)

the Church. Alas, this is very poor ground to build on. It is true that Israel at that time was set aside. Paul makes the point in Romans that the branch 'Israel' being unfruitful was set aside and the Church has benefited greatly from it.[196] But Jesus could not have intended that the word 'nation' should describe the Church - the Church cannot, in any sense, being considered a 'nation', whereas Israel is clearly considered a nation. The Matthew 21:43 text surely relates to the fact that the kingdom of God will be given to a future generation of Israel who will have accepted Jesus as Messiah. This is supported by the fact that Jesus anticipated such a day when He promised the apostles, *"Assuredly I say to you, that in the regeneration, when the Son of Man sits on the throne of His glory, you who have followed Me will also sit on twelve thrones, judging the twelve tribes of Israel"* (Matt.19:28). He clearly envisaged a day when the kingdom would be a reality and the apostles would co-reign with Him over it. This is the kingdom in question, and that will be the generation of Israel that will be blessed in it.

And anyway, how can the disobedience of Israel invalidate a legal covenant that was unconditional? Any examination of the Abrahamic Covenant or the New Covenant will conclude that there were no conditions placed on Israel. They are the beneficiaries, and the covenants are covenants of grant, that is, God has committed Himself to fulfill the conditions of the covenants. Those that maintain that the disobedience of Israel meant they failed to meet the standard of behaviour required of them, and it was within the remit of the LORD to replace Israel with the Church in respect of the Covenant are mistaken. Again, the plain understanding of Scripture does not support this.

Furthermore, under any understanding of covenant law it would be illegal to replace one beneficiary with another in a covenant where the subsequent beneficiary was not named. It must be asserted that you cannot legally, morally or spiritually transfer God's covenant with one group of people (the nation of

---

196   Michael J. Vlach. 'Has The Church Replaced Israel In God's Plan?' Conservative Theological Journal, Vol.4, (April 2000)

Israel) to another group of people (the Church). Lightfoot has rightly observed, "Even a human covenant duly confirmed is held sacred and inviolable. It cannot be set aside, it cannot be clogged with new conditions. Much more then a divine covenant." [197] Even if the Abrahamic and New Covenants were conditional, which they were not; and even if Israel failed to meet the criteria of those covenants, which they did not; it could only result in Israel losing the benefits promised – it still would not be legal for Israel or for the church to be substituted as beneficiary. Under those circumstances, the LORD might terminate the covenant with Israel and make a new covenant with believers in this later dispensation, but He cannot rewrite the covenant He made with Israel. Not only would it not be right, but it would also suggest that the LORD was dealing with an event that he did not foresee. No, His foreknowledge is perfect and every detail of the covenants reveals His will for Hebrew nation. Not only did He make at least three unconditional covenants with Israel, but at no point did He make them temporary.

But it might be suggested that God is sovereign and it is His covenant and He can do as He wishes. No, He cannot! Everything in Scripture declares that God cannot do anything that is illegal, under-handed or unrighteous. And to take this line of reasoning to its logical conclusion, how is it that those that say the Church is now the beneficiary of these Covenants, cling firmly to the idea that there are no conditions placed on the Church for remaining the beneficiary? If the LORD could put aside Israel for disobedience, how is it that the Church remains inviolable. Even a cursory glance at Church history would suggest that the Church should have been put aside, just as Israel was, and the benefits passed on to another group. No, the confidence we have is that God is omniscient, that is, He is all wise, He sees the end from the beginning. He is also immutable; He is unchanging, unchangeable and unchanged. This surely includes the sense that He does not change His mind: *"The word of the LORD endures forever"* (1 Pet. 1:25). The very chapter (Jer. 31) which includes the foundational text for the New Covenant

---

197   Rom. 11:17 ff

declares that God loves Israel with an everlasting love.[198] There is no way in which they will not enjoy future blessing from His hand. It is our confidence that what He has promised He will perform that leads us to believe that we are in possession of eternal life. If it is or becomes conditional at any time, then few of us will see heaven.

Conclusion

The texts currently used to support replacement theology fail at each point. Israel is never said to be permanently rejected by God. The titles 'Israel' and 'Jew' are never used of Gentile believers. Old Testament language can be applied to the Church without the Church becoming Israel. Believing Gentiles can become 'sons' of Abraham without becoming Jews. Spiritual equality between Jew and Gentile does not mean that there will not be a functional distinction between Jews and Gentiles in the future. Access to the New Covenant by the Church does not annul a future eschatological fulfillment with Israel.

Does it matter which doctrine is correct? Of course it does. At stake here is the character of God – is He trustworthy? Can we rely on His promises? There are three unconditional covenants for Israel to delight in - the Abrahamic, the Davidic and the New Covenant. If He has set aside the Jewish nation then He has broken His word.

Moreover, the great doctrines of the Bible are inter-connected. To be in error in one area will impact on other main streams of truth. For example the LORD is pleased to be known as the *"God of Israel"*,[199] the *"God of Abraham"*,[200] as well as the *"God of Abraham, the God of Isaac, and the God of Jacob"* (Ex. 3:6), a title which was confirmed and quoted by Jesus in Matthew 22:32. Are these titles now to be jettisoned because we have de-Judaized the covenantal God of the *T'nach*?

---

198   J.B.Lightfoot. St. Paul's Epistle to the Galatians. (London: Macmillan and co., 1874)

199   Jer. 31:3

200   There are 203 references to this Name, some of them owned by the Lord Himself.

Then there is the doctrine of the Messiah Himself, better known as 'Christology'. Supercessionism has, to a degree, reduced our appreciation of the Jewishness of Jesus. We do not give sufficient importance to the nation and history that produced the Saviour of the world. We do not draw extra light from understanding His Jewish background, for He was born of a Jewish virgin, had a Davidic lineage and taught as a travelling Rabbi.

The greatest impact, it would appear, is on 'eschatology', that is the doctrine of the end times. Since, under replacement teaching the Jewish nation has been set aside, there can be no expectation of their restoration. Under supercessionism there will be no return of the nation to their land, no future Temple and no Jewish evangelists on a mission to the Gentiles. This view of future events will require a manipulation of all the Scriptures that deal with the rapture of the Church, the period of tribulation, the return of Christ, the Millennial kingdom and judgments to come.

Those who hold a supercessionist outlook must find the Old Testament a very uncomfortable book, for it makes it clear that it is impossible for the Jewish nation to be separated from God, for they are *"inscribed on the palms of (His) hands"* (Isaiah 49.16). As long as He occupies the throne of heaven, the position of the Jewish nation must remain secure, and the Church can remain confident in their covenant keeping God. Because He will keep His covenant promises to Israel, we can be assured that our future in His care is safe, because that is the blanket of blessing under which we rest.

Concluding Summary
The Abrahamic Covenant

We began by suggesting that the purpose of God, formed before the foundation of the world, was that He was set on creating a living organism with which He could have fellowship. He was aiming to bring into being, a complex and unique group of living creatures, who together would be able to receive and give love. And because this unit, which we can now identify as the Church, would be made up of many and varied individuals, it would be of such caliber and stature that it would be a worthy object of the love and attention of the Godhead.

The Abrahamic Covenant was the beginning of that process. Abraham was to be father of the faithful –'the faithful' being drawn from all nations. Abraham, elected by God to be the door through which abundant blessings would flow, began the process. He believed God and was imputed righteous. From his loins came the nation that would bring the knowledge of God, understand fellowship with God and recognize the righteousness of God.

The Mosaic Covenant

This covenant was designed to continue the underlying purpose of God. The nation was to be trained in righteousness and fellowship. God dwelt among them – they knew His presence – they heard His word – they had His protection. The covenant not only laid on them obedience to the righteous requirements of the LORD, but they were also commanded to love Him. They were being trained to take their place in new entity that was the ultimate goal of God.

The Land Covenant

The land covenant which imposed conditions on the occupation of the Promised Land was designed to encourage the faithfulness of Israel. Be faithful and be safe in your homeland; but if you apostatize you will be evicted.

The Davidic Covenant

This covenant, while initially being part of the plan of God to bring to Israel the Messiah, the promised seed of Abraham, was also a great encouragement to them through dark times. While this covenant was in place (and it was always in place) they always had hope. They could anticipate a Deliverer, a Son of David to come and rescue them.

The New Covenant

This was promised to the nation during one of its darkest periods. When things were at their worst God made a covenant promise that there would be a day when the nation would come into the fullness of the blessing of the Abrahamic Covenant. This was where the Abrahamic Covenant was pointing – to the blessing of God upon the nation, which would also be the catalyst for blessing for the whole of humankind.

The Messiah

Jesus of Nazareth, conceived of the Holy Spirit, born of a virgin, was the 'seed' of Abraham, and the instrument by which the Abrahamic Covenant could be fulfilled. He was a law abiding Hebrew who obeyed and fulfilled the Mosaic Covenant in every aspect. He knew His covenants and prophesied that His rejection would activate the Land Covenant, and Israel would lose their temple, city and homeland. But He also knew that a future quickening of both the Davidic and New Covenants would bring blessing to the nation and they would again occupy the land and enjoy fellowship with the God that had chosen them. In the meantime, His death, the great act that allowed an immediate activation of the New Covenant, was to be of such a magnitude that the salvation of God would reach the ends of the earth. So any individual who recognizes who He is and what He has done has access to the blessings that are available under the Abrahamic and New Covenants.

The Church

Those believers who now make up the members of the body of the Messiah, the Church, rejoice that God elected a man, 'cut' a covenant with him, trained the nation that came from him by means of a conditional covenant, and offered them unconditional covenants by which the means of salvation could proliferate to all people. The members of the Church recognize that the benefits of salvation come to them through the death of the Jewish Messiah, and they have eternal life because they can share in the blessings of the Abrahamic and New Covenants.

Consequently they acknowledge the debt they owe to the Hebrew nation, and are happy to confess that Israel remains God's chosen people, and they still feature in His future plans.

The Nation of Israel

The Scriptures teach that they will yet come into the fullness of the Abrahamic Covenant; they will possess the Land; they will know success in a kingdom ruled under in fulfillment of the Davidic Covenant; for the nation will be saved on the basis of the New Covenant.

A Last Diagram

Since the Abrahamic, Davidic and New Covenants are eternal and unconditional, as also is the land aspect of the Abrahamic Covenant, we can picture their validity as follows:

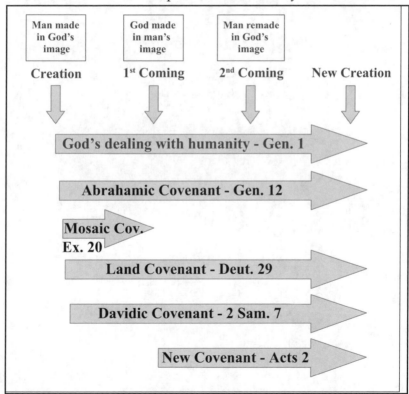

179

Bibliography

Showers, Renold. E. There really is a difference. Bellmawr, NJ: Friends of Israel Gospel Ministry, 1990

The Jewish Study Bible Edited by Adele Berlin and Marc Zvi Brettler. Oxford University Press, Inc. New York, 2004

The JPS Torah Commentary – Exodus Nahum M. Sarna. Jewish Publication Society. Philadelphia, 1991

Keil, C.F. & Delitzsch, F, Commentary on the Old Testament, Electronic Edition. Peabody: Hendrickson Publishers Inc., 2002

The Babylonian Talmud. Trans.Rabbi Dr. I. Epstein. Brooklyn: Soncino Press, 1938

Sheldon, Bryan W. The Messiah and the Feasts of Israel Port Colborne, ON. Gospel Folio Press, 2006

Garrard, Alec. The Splendour of the Temple. Grand Rapids: Kregel Publications, 1997

Patterson, Sinclair. The Great Doctrines of the Bible. Chicago: Moody Press, 1974

The Works of Josephus. Trans. William Whiston. Peabody: Hendrickson Publishers Inc., 2001

Schurer, E. A History of the Jewish People in the time of Jesus Christ. Edinburgh. T & T Clark. 1890

Chafer, Lewis Sperry. Systematic Theology Grand Rapids, MI: Kregel Publications. 1993

Lightfoot, J.B. St. Paul's Epistle to the Galatians. London: Macmillan and co. 1874

Neusner, Jacob. The Mishnah, a New Translation. London. Yale University Press. 1988

There are 17 references to this identification, including some which speak of the God of Abraham, Isaac and Jacob.

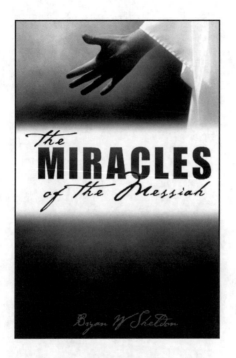

The Miracles of the Messiah
Bryan W. Sheldon
Item #: B-7396

Almost two millennia ago, a group of Jewish leaders plotted the execution of a young man, Jesus of Nazareth. The death of this young Jew has had implications for the whole of humankind ever since. *The Miracles of the Messiah* re-examines the events of those days and places them in the culture of the period.

GOSPEL FOLIO PRESS
I WILL PUBLISH THE NAME OF THE LORD

304 Killaly St. West | Port Colborne | ON | L3K 6A6 | Canada
1 800 952 2382 | E-mail: info@gospelfolio.com | www.gospelfolio.com

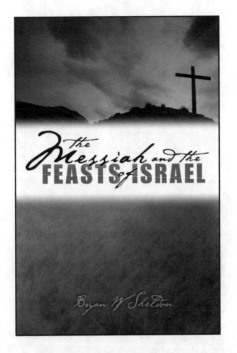

The Messiah and the Feasts of Israel
Bryan W. Sheldon
Item #: B-7590

The Feasts of the Lord were placed in the calendar of the Hebrew nation as a prophetic timetable of God's redemptive plan. Israel, in celebrating the spring cycle of feasts was compelled to look back to their deliverance from Egyptian slavery and the giving of the Torah. But these feasts were not only memorials of great acts of God in the past, but also finger-posts to future events when Messiah would come.

GOSPEL FOLIO PRESS
I WILL PUBLISH THE NAME OF THE LORD

304 Killaly St. West | Port Colborne | ON | L3K 6A6 | Canada
1 800 952 2382 | E-mail: info@gospelfolio.com | www.gospelfolio.com